ORGANIZATIONAL BEHAVIOUR

ORGANIZATIONAL BEHAVIOUR

By

Dr. M. Karthikeyan
Assistant Professor
Department of Cooperatives
Faculty of Business & Economics
Hawassa University
Hawassa
Email: mkeya2003@gmail.com
mkeya2003@yahoo.com

&

Dr. Assefa Gebre
Associate Professor
College of Agriculture
Adama University
Ethiopia

DPH

DISCOVERY PUBLISHING HOUSE PVT. LTD.
NEW DELHI-110 002

Published by:

Tilak Wasan

DISCOVERY PUBLISHING HOUSE PVT. LTD.
4383/4A, Ansari Road, Darya Ganj
New Delhi-110 002 (India)
Phone : +91-11-23279245, 43596064-65
Fax : +91-11-23253475
E-mail : parul.wasan@gmail.com
discoverypublishinghouse@gmail.com
web : www.discoverypublishinggroup.com

***First Edition:* 2012**
ISBN: 978-93-5056-110-2

Organizational Behaviour

Printed at:
Shree Balaji Art Press
Delhi

Preface

Dear Readers! It is our pleasure to introduce the textbook on ***Organizational Behaviour*** to you. It has been designed in a manner so as to help you understand the basic concepts of organization, and organization behaviour. We have tried to cover basic aspects on organization behaviour concepts, group dynamics, organizational communication, motivation, leadership and organization development.

This work is based on our experience as teacher, practitioner, trainer and researcher in the field of cooperatives and management for more than 15 years. The present work is based on undergraduate programme curriculum and outcome of our teaching and research experience, and articles published in reputed journals. This book will be very much useful to the students of undergraduate, professionals, and the trainers who are working in various training establishments. We have drawn the inputs from various materials— papers, journals, books and we have consulted several of our friends, colleagues and field experts. We are ever grateful and thankful to them for their immense support and healthy criticism. We hope that the readers of this book will get knowledge on organization behavior issues. Any useful comments, suggestions to improve the present version are welcome and solicited from the readers. We are thankful and grateful to Parul Wasan, Discovery Publishing House Pvt. Ltd., New Delhi for publishing this book neatly under his renowned label for the knowledge community.

M. KARTHIKEYAN

ASSEFA GEBRE

Contents

	Preface	
1.	Organization	1
2.	Organizational Behaviour	18
3.	Basic Psychological Process	35
4.	Motivation	63
5.	Group Dynamics	77
6.	Communication	94
7.	Perception and Attitudes	101
8.	Organization Goals	110
9.	Organization Control	120
10.	Influence, Power, Authority, Leadership	133
11.	Organization Conflict	145
12.	Organization Development	155
	References	*175*
	Index	*177*

1

Organization

What is an Organization?

Robbins Stephan P. defined organization as a consciously coordinated social entity, with a relatively identifiable boundary, that functions on a relatively continuous basis to achieve a common goal or set of goals. Let us break it down into its more relevant parts.

The words 'consciously coordinated' imply management. 'Social entity' means that the unit is composed of people or groups of people who interact with each other. The interaction patterns that people follow in an organization do not just emerge; rather, they are premeditated. Therefore, because organizations are social entities, the interaction patterns of their members must be balanced and harmonized to minimize redundancy yet ensure that critical tasks are being completed. The result assumes explicitly the need for coordinating the interaction patterns of people.

An organization has a relatively identifiable boundary. This boundary can change over time, and it may not always be perfectly clear, but a definable boundary must exist in order to distinguish members from non-members. It tends to be achieved by explicit or implicit contracts between members and their organizations. In most employment relationships, there is an implicit contract where work is exchanged for pay. In social or voluntary organizations, members contribute in turn for prestige, social interaction, or the satisfaction of helping others. But every organization has a boundary that differentiates who is and who is not part of that organization.

People in an organization have some continuing bond. This bond, of course, does not mean lifelong membership. On the contrary, organizations face constant change in their membership, although while they are members, the people in the organization participate with some degrees of regularity.

Finally Organizations exist to achieve something. These "some-things" are goals, and they usually are either unattainable by individuals working alone or, if attainable individually, are achieved more efficiently through group effort. While it is not necessary for all members to endorse the organizations goals fully, the definition implies general agreement with the mission of the organization.

According to Chester I Barnard's classic definition, an organization is "a system of consciously coordinated activities or forces of two or more persons". Embodied in the conscious coordination aspect of this definition are four common denominators of all organizations— coordination of effort, a common goal, division of labour, and a hierarchy of authority (Fig.1.1) Organization theorists refer to these factors as the organization's structure.

Coordination of effort is achieved through formulation and enforcement of policies, rules, and regulations. Division of labour occurs when the common goal is pursued by individuals performing separate but related tasks. The hierarchy of authority, also called the chain of command, is a control mechanism dedicated to making sure the right people do the right things at the right time. Historically, managers have maintained the integrity of the hierarchy of authority by adhering to the unity of command principle. The unity of command principle specifies that each employee should report to only one manager. Otherwise, inefficiency would prevail because of conflicting orders and lack of personal accountability. (Indeed, these are problems in today's more fluid and flexible organizations based on innovations such as cross functional and self-managed teams.) Managers in the

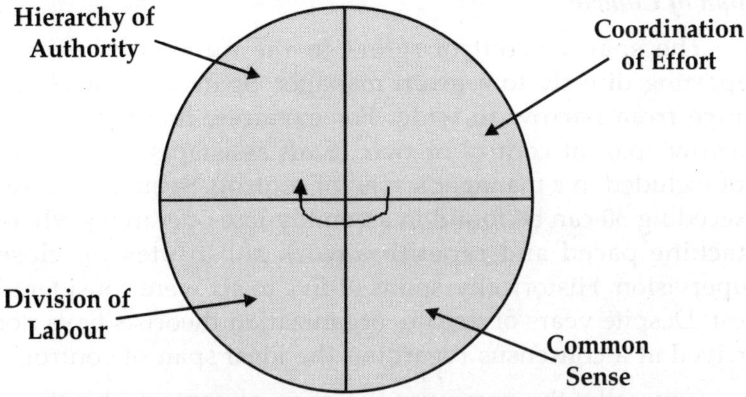

Fig. 1.1: **Four characteristics common to all organizations**

hierarchy of authority also administer rewards and punishments. When the four factors in figure 1.1 operate in concert, the dynamic entity called an organization exists.

Organization Charts

An organization chart is a graphic representation of formal authority and division of labour relationships. To the casual observer, the term organization chart means the family tree like pattern of boxes and lines posted on workplace walls. Within each box one usually finds the names and titles of current position holders. To organization theorists, however, organization charts reveal much more. A partial organization reveals four basic dimensions of organizational structure: hierarchy of authority (who reports to whom); division of labour; spans of control; line and staff positions.

Hierarchy of Authority

A formal hierarchy of authority also delineates the official communication network.

Division of Labour

In addition to showing the chain of command, simple organization chart indicates extensive division of labour. At each successively lower level in the organization, jobs become more specialized.

Span of Control

The span of control refers to the number of people reporting directly to a given manager. Spans of control can range from narrow to wide. For example, there may be a narrow span of control of two. (Staff assistants usually are not included in a manager's span of control). Spans of control exceeding 30 can be found in assembly-line operations where machine paced and repetitive work substitutes for close supervision. Historically, spans of five to six were considered best. Despite years of debate, organization theorists have not arrived at a consensus regarding the ideal span of control.

Generally, the narrower the span of control, the closer the supervision and the higher the administrative costs as a result of a higher manager-to-worker ratio. Recent emphasis on leanness and administrative efficiency dictates spans of control as wide as possible but guarding against inadequate supervision and lack of coordination. Wider spans also complement the trend toward greater worker autonomy and empowerment.

Line and Staff Positions

An organization chart also distinguishes between line and staff positions. Line managers occupy formal decision-making positions within the chain of command. Line positions generally are connected by solid lines on organization charts. Dotted lines indicate staff relationships. Staff personnel do background research and provide technical advice and recommendations to their line managers, who have the authority to make decisions. Apart from supervising the work of their own staff assistants, they have no line authority over other organizational members.

What is an organization structure?

The definition of organization recognizes the need for formally coordinating the interaction patterns of organization members. Organization structure defines how tasks are allocated, who reports to whom, and the formal coordinating mechanisms and interaction patterns that will be allowed. We define organization's structure as having three components: complexity, formalization and centralization.

Complexity

Complexity considers the extent of differentiation within the organization. This includes the degree of specialization or division of labour, the number of people in the organization's hierarchy and the extent to which the organization's units are dispersed geographically.

Formalization

The degree to which an organization relies on rules and procedures to direct the behaviour of employees is formalization. Some organizations operate with a minimum of such standardized guidelines and; others, some of which are even quite small in size, have all kinds of regulations instructing employees as to what they can do and cannot do.

Centralization

Centralization considers where the locus of decision-making authority lies. In some organizations, decision-making is highly decentralized. Problems flow upward, and the senior executives choose appropriate action. In other cases, decision making is decentralized. It is important to recognize that as with complexity and formalization, an organization is centralized or decentralized. Centralization and decentralization represent two extremes on a continuum. Organizations tend to be centralized or tend to be decentralized. The placement of an organization on the continuum, however, is one of the major factors in determining what type of structure exists.

What is an organization Design?

Organization design emphasizes the management side of organization theory. Organization design is concerned with constructing and changing an organizations structure to achieve the organization's goals.

What is an Organizational Theory?

Organization Theory is the discipline that studies the structure and design of organizations. Organization Theory refers to both the descriptive and prescriptive aspects of the discipline. It describes how organizations are actually structured and offers suggestions on how they can be constructed to improve their effectiveness.

What is the difference between the subject matter of organization theory and that of organizational behaviour?

Contrasting Organization Theory and Organizational Behaviour

It might be helpful in this section to differentiate Organization Theory (OT) from that of Organizational behaviour (OB). A brief comparison of the two terminologies can assist students of management and organizations in understanding the terminologies' different terrains and as well as their areas of overlap.

Organizational behaviour (OB) takes a micro view emphasizing individuals and small groups. It focuses on behaviour in organizations and a narrow set of employee performance and attitude variables — employee productivity, absenteeism, and turnover and job satisfaction are those most frequently looked at. Individual behaviour topics studied in organizational behaviour include perception, values, learning, motivation, and personality. Group topics include roles, status, leadership, power, communication and conflict.

Organizational behaviour is a field of study that investigates the impact that individuals, groups and structure have on behaviour within the organization for the purpose of applying such knowledge toward improving organizational effectiveness. Breaking down the definition: Organizational behaviour is a field of study. This statement means that it is a distinct area of expertise with a common body of knowledge. What does it study? It studies three determinants of behaviour in organizations— individuals, groups and structure. In addition OB applies the knowledge gained about individuals, groups and the effect of structure on behaviour in order to make organizations work more effectively.

In contrast, *Organization theory* (OT) takes a macro perspective. Its unit of analysis is the organization itself or its primary subunits. Organizational theory focuses on the behaviour of organizations and uses a broader definition of organizational effectiveness. Organizational theory is concerned not only with employee performance and attitudes but with the overall organization's ability to adapt and achieve goals.

The micro-macro distinction creates some overlap. For instance structural factors have an impact on employee behaviour. So students of OB should consider the structure-behaviour relationships. Similarly, some micro topics are relevant to the study of OT. But where micro and macro issues overlap, their emphasis is often different. For instance, the topic of conflict in OB tends to focus on interpersonal and intragroup conflicts that derive from personality differences and poor communication. Conflict when studied by organization theorists, emphasizes problems of inter-unit coordination. While the student of OB is likely to see all conflicts as 'people' problems, the student of OT tends to see the same conflict as resulting from flaws in the organizations design. The issue, of course, is not that one is right and the other is wrong. Rather OB and OT merely emphasize different level of organizational analysis.

The Evolution of Organizational Theory

The current state of organization theory is the result of an evolutionary process. Over a period of many decades, academics and practitioners from diverse backgrounds and with diverse perspectives have studied and analyzed organizations. The purpose of this chapter is to overview these contributions briefly and demonstrate how we got to where we are today. The major theme throughout this review is that current organization theories reflect a cumulative developmental pattern. Theories have been introduced, evaluated, and refined over time; new insights tend to reflect the limitations of earlier theories. So if you want to understand what is happening today in organization theory, you need to look back along the path from which it has come.

Developing a Framework

The real 'action' in organization theory has taken place since the turn of the century. There were a few major pre-twentieth century. However, the real problem lies in developing a framework that can adequately demonstrate the evolutionary nature of contemporary organization theory. That is, how do you organize organization theory?

It has been suggested that there are two underlying dimensions in the evolution of organization theory and that each dimension, in turn, has opposed perspectives. The first dimension reflects that organizations are systems. Prior to about 1960, organization theory tended to be dominated by a closed system perspective. Organizations were seen as essentially autonomous and sealed off from their environment. Beginning around 1960, however, organization theory began to take on a distinctly open-system perspective. Analyses that previously had placed primary focus on the internal characteristics of organization gave way to approaches that emphasized the importance for the organization of events and processes external to it. The second dimension deals with the ends of organization structure. Here again are two opposed positions. The rational perspective argues that the structure of an organization is conceived as a vehicle to effectively achieve specified objectives. In contrast, the social perspective emphasizes that structure is primarily the result of the conflicting forces by the organization's constituents who seek power and control. Table 1.1 depicts the evolution of contemporary organization theory along the systems and ends dimensions. The result is four theoretical classifications-labeled type 1 through 4. The time frame for each is obviously an approximation. The section will introduce a couple of theorists who fall outside these time periods. Overall, however, the data shown in table 1.1represent useful guides for understanding the evolution of organization theory. The early approaches to organization theory in this century conceived of organizations as mechanical devices to achieve goals. Attention focuses on achieving efficiency in internal functions of the organization. We will use the label type 1 to describe theorists in this era.

Table 1.1: Evolution of contemporary organization theory

Approximate time frame	1900-1930	1930-1960	1960-1975	1975- ?
System perspective	Closed	Closed	Open	Open
Ends perspective	Rational	Social	Rational	Social
Central theme	Mechanical efficiency	People and human relations	Contingency designs	Power and politics
Theoretical classification	Type 1	Type 2	Type 3	Type 4

Source: Robins, Stephens P. Organization Theory: structure, Design and Application 1990), p. 31.

Type 2 theorists operated under closed system assumptions but emphasized the informal relations and non-economic motives operating in organizations. Organizations were not well oiled and perfectly predictable machines. Management could design formal relationships, rules, and the like, but there were informal patterns of communication, status, norms, and friendships created to meet the social needs of organization members.

Rationality returns again in *Type 3*. Theorists during the 1960s and early 1970s saw organizations as the vehicle for achieving goals. They concentrated on size, technology, and environmental uncertainty as the major contingency variables that determined what the right structure for an organization should be. Type 3 theorists argued that properly aligning structure to its contingency variables would facilitate the achievement of the organization's goals. Conversely, implementation of the wrong structure could threaten the organization's survival.

Finally, our current approach to understanding organizations is being strongly influenced by *Type 4* theorists. The social perspective has made a comeback but in an open-system framework. The result is the viewpoint that structure is not the rational effort by managers to create the most effective structure but rather the outcome of the political struggles among coalitions within the organization for control.

TYPE 1 THEORISTS

The type 1 theorists,

- ❖ known as the classical school;
- ❖ developed universal principles or models that would apply in all situations;
- ❖ perceived organizations as closed systems created to achieve goals efficiently.

1. Frederick Taylor and Scientific Management

Frederick Winslow Taylor's in 1911

- ❖ Published principles of scientific management.
- ❖ Set out to correct the situation by applying the scientific method to jobs on the shop floor.
- ❖ There is 'one best way' in which each job should be done and therefore generate work design.
- ❖ Proposed four principles of scientific management so as to increase productivity through:
  1. The replacement of rule-of-thumb methods for determining each element of a worker's job with scientific determination.
  2. The scientific selection and training of workers.
  3. The cooperation of management and labour to accomplish work objectives, in accordance with the scientific method.

4. A more equal division of responsibility between managers (doing the planning and supervising) and workers (doing the execution).

2. Henri Fayol and Principles of Organization

Henry Fayol

❖ Sought to develop general principles applicable to all managers at all levels of the organization and to describe the functions a manager should perform.

❖ Proposed fourteen principles that he argued were universally applicable and could be taught in schools and universities.

❖ Many of these organizing principles, though lacking in universality, certainly are widely followed by managers today.

Note: Refer the fourteen principles from any management book.

3. Max Weber and Bureaucracy

Max Weber

❖ Developed a structural model that, he called this ideal structure bureaucracy, which he argued, was the most efficient means by which organizations can achieve their ends. Bureaucracy was characterized by:

- Division of labour
- A clear authority hierarchy
- Formal selection procedures
- Detailed rules and regulations, and
- Impersonal relationships.

Weber's description of bureaucracy became the design prototype for the structures of most of today's large organizations.

4. Ralph Davis and Rational Planning

Ralph C. Davis

❖ Stated that the primary objective of a business firm is economic service.

- No business can survive if it doesn't provide economic value.
- This economic value is generated by the activities members engage in to create the organization's objectives to its results.
- It is management's job to group these activities together in such a way as to form the structure of the organization.
- Concluded, that the structure of the organization is contingent upon the organization's objectives.

Management's formal planning determines the organization's objectives. These objectives determine:

- the development of structure;
- the flow of authority; and
- other relationships.

TYPE 2 THEORISTS

The common theme among type 2 theorists is:

- Recognized the social nature of organizations.
- Type 2 theorists represent a human counterpoint to type 1's machine view.

1. Elton Mayo and the Hawthorne Studies

- Experiments undertaken at Western Electric Company's Hawthorne Works in Cicero, Illinois, between 1924 and 1927.
- These Hawthorne studies were to examine the effect of various illumination levels on workers productivity.
- The engineers concluded that illumination intensity clearly was not directly related to group productivity, but they could not explain the behaviour they had witnessed.
- Later studies' result indicated that the wage incentive plan was less of a determining factor on a worker's output than were group pressure and acceptance and the concomitant security.

- Social norms of the group were concluded to be the key determinants of individual work behaviour.

It was recommended that managers would no longer consider the issue of organization design without including effects on work groups, employee attitudes, and manager employee relationships.

2. Chester Barnard and Cooperative Systems

Chester Barnard is credited for:

- The conclusion that organizations are cooperative systems.
- Organizations are composed of tasks and people that have to be maintained at an equilibrium state.
- Challenged the classical view that authority flowed from the top down by arguing that authority should be defined in terms of the response of the subordinate.
- Introduced the role of the informal organization to organization theory.
- Proposed that the manager's major roles were to facilitate communication and to stimulate subordinates to high levels of effort.

3. Douglas McGregor and Theory X, Theory Y

Douglas McGregor's thesis shows that there are two distinct views of human beings:

(a) One basically negative — Theory X and

(b) the other basically positive — Theory Y.

Under Theory X, four assumptions are held by managers:

1. Employees inherently dislike work and, whenever possible, will attempt to avoid it.
2. Since employees dislike work, they must be coerced, controlled or threatened with punishment to achieve desired goals.
3. Employees will shirk responsibilities and seek formal direction whenever possible.

4. Most workers place security above all other factors associated with work and will display little ambition.

In contrast to these negative views of human beings, McGregor listed four other assumptions that he called Theory Y:

1. Employees can view work as being as natural as rest or play.
2. Human beings will exercise self-direction and self-control if they are committed to the objectives.
3. The average person can learn to accept, even seek, responsibility.
4. Creativity — that is, the ability to make good decisions - is widely dispersed throughout the population and is not necessarily the sole province of those in managerial functions.

What are the implications of McGregor's Theory X and Theory Y to organization theory? McGregor argued that Theory Y assumptions were preferable and that they should guide managers in the way they designed their organizations and motivated their employees.

4. Warren Bennis and the Death of Bureaucracy

Warren Bennis

- Claimed that bureaucracy's centralized decision-making impersonal submission to authority, and narrow division of labour was being replaced by decentralization and democratic structures organized around flexible groups.
- Argued the other extreme conditions now pointed to flexible autocracies as the ideal organizational form.

TYPE 3 THEORISTS

This was a contingency approach.

1. Herbert Simon and Principles Backlash

Herbert Simon

- Recognized in the 1940s that type 1 principles would have to give way to a contingency approach.

- ❖ Noted that most classical principles were nothing more than proverbs, and many contradicted each other.
- ❖ Argued that organization theory needed to go beyond superficial and oversimplified principles to a study of the conditions under which competing principles were applicable.
- ❖ The 1950s and 1960s tended to be dominated by simplistic principles — of both the mechanistic and humanistic variety.

2. Katz and Kahn's Environmental Perspective

Katz and Kahn's book

- ❖ Provided a convincing description of the advantages of an open systems perspective for examining the important relations of an organization with its environment.
- ❖ The need for organizations to adapt to a changing environment if they are to survive.

Numerous other theorists have investigated the environment-structure relationship and conclude that no current discussion of organization theory would be complete without a thorough assessment of environment as a major contingency factor influencing the preferred form of structure.

3. The Case for Technology

Research in the 1960s by Joan Woodward and Charles Perrow, as well as the conceptual framework offered by James Thompson, have made an impressive case for the importance of technology in determining the appropriate structure for an organization. As with environment, no contemporary discussion of organization theory would be complete without consideration of technology and the need for managers to match structure with technology.

4. The Aston group and Organization Size

In addition to advocates of environment and technology, the type 3 theorists include those who advocate organization size as an important factor influencing structure. This position has been most zealously argued by researchers associated with the University of Aston in Great Britain. Large organizations have been shown to have many common structural components. So, too, have small organizations. Maybe most important, the evidence suggests that certain of these components follow an established pattern as organizations expand in size. Such evidence has proven valuable to managers in helping them make organization-design decisions as their organizations grew.

TYPE 4 THEORISTS

The most recent approach to organization theory focuses on the political nature of organizations. The early formation of this position was made by James March and Herbert Simon, but it has been extensively refined by Jeffrey Pfeffer.

1. March and Simon's Cognitive Limits to Rationality

March and Simon challenged the classical notion of rational or optimum decisions. They argued that most decision-makers selected satisfactory alternatives—alternatives that were good enough. Only in exceptional cases would they be concerned with the discovery and selection of optimal alternatives. March and Simon called for a revised model of organization Theory 1 very different from the rational cooperative systems view. This revised model would recognize the limits of a decision-maker's rationality and acknowledge the presence of conflicting goals.

2. Pfeffer's Organizations as Political Arenas

Jeffrey Pfeffer has built on March and Simon's work to create a model of organization theory that encompasses power coalitions, inherent conflict over goals, and organizational-design decisions that favor the self interest of those in power. Pfeffer proposes that control in organizations becomes an end rather than merely a means to rational goals such as efficient production of output. Organizations are coalitions composed of varying groups and individuals with different demands.

An organization's design represents the result of the power struggles by these diverse coalitions. Pfeffer argues that if we want to understand how and why organizations are designed the way they are, we need to assess the preferences and interests of those in the organization who have influences over the design decisions. This view is currently very much in vogue.

Summary

- An organization has a relatively identifiable boundary. This boundary can change over time, and it may not always be perfectly clear, but a definable boundary must exist in order to distinguish members from non-members.
- An organization chart is a graphic representation of formal authority and division of labour relationships.
- Organization structure defines how tasks are allocated, who reports to whom, and the formal coordinating mechanisms and interaction patterns that will be allowed.
- Organizational behaviour takes a micro view emphasizing individuals and small groups. It focuses on behaviour in organizations and a narrow set of employee performance and attitude variables.
- Organization theory takes a macro perspective. Its unit of analysis is the organization itself or its primary sub-units. Organizational theory focuses on the behaviour of organizations and uses a broader definition of organizational effectiveness.

Self-Learning Activity

Try to answer the following questions on your own:

1. What is an organization?
2. Write short notes on: Span of Control.
3. Contrast organization theory and organization behaviour?

2

Organizational Behaviour

Why do people behave the way they do? What causes different people to react differently to the same situation? Why are some organizations more successful than others, even though they appear to be managed in the same manner? And why do managers spend so much of their time trying to 'figure out what makes people tick'? All of these questions and more are the substance of what organizational behaviour is all about. An understanding of the behaviour of people in organizations has become increasingly important as more and more of us find ourselves involved with organizations and the management of people, not only at work, but in all facets of our lives.

Even though one might not be a manager, it is still important to understand as much as possible about how people behave at work if we want to make our organizational lives more pleasant and productive. Consider the following situations as a few examples that illustrate common patterns of behaviour in organizations:

1. The manager of an accounting department finds that the accounting clerks are beginning to make errors in calculations that were seldom made before.
2. A police chief notices an improvement in job attitudes of patrolmen after their supervisor retired and was replaced.

3. The foreman in a production department is faced with consistently high absenteeism on Mondays and Fridays.
4. The president of an organization realizes that the vice-presidents seem reluctant to offer new ideas on how the company should be managed.
5. A new employee in the typing pool notices that none of the other typists are acting very friendly.
6. A college dean notices improved communication and greater faculty commitment after reorganization of the academic unit.
7. The committee chairman of a local volunteer fund raising drive is informed that most of the volunteers have requested to be dropped from the committee after the current drive is over, even though more funds have been raised than ever before.
8. The personnel manager of a manufacturing organization notices that the company is having increased difficulty recruiting new production workers, even though their wage rate is the highest in the local area.

These examples illustrate the need for understanding behaviour at all levels of management and in all types of organizations. In virtually all cases, it is desirable to have the ability both to solve problems and to prevent them from occurring. To have this ability we must have an understanding of why people behave as they do. If one has the ability and knowledge to understand why people behave the way they do, then foresight, anticipation, and prevention of problems become more probable.

MANAGER AS AN ANALYST

Learning requires studying organizational relationships, patterns of behaviour, and theories about organizational behaviour. The ultimate goal is an increased understanding of cause and effect relationships, i.e., the 'whys' of behaviour in organizations. One of the objectives in studying this course is to increase the students' ability to think analytically about organizational behaviour. Analytical thinking results from a clear understanding of the (1) content of various theories and (2) manner in which they can be applied. To get from (1) to (2) requires an awareness of the research available for a given theory. In other words, we must learn how the theory works, when it works, and most importantly, why it works.

NATURE AND SCOPE OF ORGANIZATIONAL BEHAVIOUR

Using our definition of the study of organizational behaviour as the study of why people behave the way they do in organizations, it is safe to say that the field has existed for many thousands of years. People have always attempted to understand and predict how other people will behave in work situations of all types, but the magnitude of this need is largely determined by the sizes and types of organizations in existence. By size we mean the number of individuals working together toward a specific set of goals; by type we mean whether membership in the organization is voluntary or involuntary.

Nature of Organizational Behaviour

Organizational behaviour, (OB), is an interdisciplinary field dedicated to better understanding and managing people at work. By definition, organizational behaviour is both research- and application-oriented. Three basic levels of analysis in OB are individual, group, and organizational. OB draws upon a diverse array of disciplines, including psychology, management, sociology, organization theory, social psychology statistics, anthropology, general systems theory, economics, information technology, political science, vocational counseling, human stress management, psychometrics, ergonomics, decision theory and ethics. Organizational behaviour is not a discipline but rather an eclectic field of study that integrates the behavioural sciences (psychology, sociology, anthropology, etc.) into the study of human behaviour within organizations.

Although organizational behaviour uses the relatively exact tools of mathematics and statistics in its research methods, it is far from an exact science itself. Because it is such a young field of inquiry, at least in terms of the use of scientific answers to specific organizational problems. This can be quite frustrating for the teacher as well as the student of organizational behaviour. Managers feel a need for precise answers as they face important day-to-day problems; teachers, on the other hand, knowing that organizational behaviour is a "soft" area, are reluctant (or should be) to be too precise in teaching "how-to-do-it" methods. The net result is a feeling of irritation by the student (why study something that won't give me an exact answer?) and feeling of inadequacy by the teacher (I wish I had something more concrete to give them). But to learn that human behaviour in organizations is not an exact science is, in itself, a significant realization. One of the failings of the scientific management movement was its belief that human behaviour was easily predicted. So while the field of organizational behaviour may be inexact, it is realistic.

Organizational Behaviour: An Art or a Science?

Whether or not organizational behaviour (or management, for that matter) is an art or a science is an age-old question with a relatively obvious answer— it is both. The knowledge about human behaviour in organizations lies toward the science end of the continuum; the skill in applying that knowledge clearly leans toward the art end, recognizing that individual differences in managerial style can vary considerably.

Scope of Organizational Behaviour

Since we earlier defined organizational behaviour very broadly as "the scientific study of why people behave the way they do in organization," it follows that its scope is quite wide-wide enough, in fact, that it is necessary for us to set some limits on the subject area so that our discussion can be reasonably contained.

In many situations it may be permissible to use the terms organizational behaviour and management interchangeably. A good case can be made for doing so since both involve in the study of organizations. It is sometimes convenient to divide the term management into two areas— the behavioural side and the managerial process side. The behavioural side concerns why people behave the way they do in organization; the process side, which has its origins in the classical 'principles of management,' concerns the managerial processes of planning, organizing, controlling etc., as well as the management science (quantitative) aspects of management. While it is convenient to make this arbitrary division, it must be understood that organizational behaviour is affected by management processes.

CONTRIBUTING DISCIPLINES TO THE OB FIELD

Psychology

Psychology is the science that seeks to measure, explain, and sometimes change the behaviour of humans and other animals. Psychologists concern themselves with studying and attempting to understand individual behaviour. Those who have contributed to and to contribute to add to the knowledge of OB are learning theorists, personality theorists, counseling psychologists, and most important, individual and organizational psychologists.

Early industrial/organizational psychologists concerned themselves with the problems of fatigue, boredom, and other factors relevant to working conditions that could impede efficient performance. More recently, their contributions have been expanded to include learning, perception, personality, emotions, training, leadership effectiveness, needs and motivational forces, job satisfaction, decision-making processes, performance appraisals, attitude measurement, employee selection techniques, work design and job stress.

Sociology

While psychology focuses on the individual, sociology studies people in relation to their fellow human beings.

Specifically, sociologists have made their contributions to OB through study of group behaviour in organizations, particularly formal and complex organizations. Some of the areas of in OB that have received valuable input from sociologists are group dynamics, design of work teams, organization culture, formal organization theory and structure, organizational technology, communications and conflict.

Social Psychology

Social psychology blends concepts from both psychology and sociology. It focuses on the influence of people on one another. One of the major areas under considerable investigation by social psychologists has been change — how to implement it and how to reduce barriers to its acceptance. In addition, we find social psychologists making contributions in the areas of measuring, understanding, and changing attitudes; communication patterns; building trust; the ways in which group activities can satisfy individual needs; and group decision-making processes.

Anthropology

Anthropology is the study of societies to learn about human beings and their activities. For instance, Anthropologists work on cultures and environments has helped us understand differences in fundamental values, attitudes and behaviour between people in different countries and within different organizations. Much of our current understanding of organizational culture, organizational environments, and differences between national cultures is the result of the work of anthropologists or those using their methods.

Political Science

Political science studies the behaviour of individuals and groups within the political environment. Specific topics of concern include the structuring of conflict, allocation of power, and how people manipulate power for individual self-interest.

ORGANIZATIONAL BEHAVIOUR AND YOUR CAREER

It was mentioned earlier that organizational behaviour is not a discipline in itself. Similarly, organizational behaviour is not a functional area within organizations (i.e., one does not find a vice-president of organizational behaviour in companies). It is a tool area that can be applied across functional lines and should be useful to anyone who interacts in a work-setting with other people (which includes just about everyone).

The roll of organizational behaviour in your own career development can best be understood by examining the differences between technical education and managerial education. Your first job will be that of a technical specialist, i.e. actually doing a specific set of tasks for which you were trained. However, at some point in your career, you will likely become a manager or supervisor. The technical skills you have studied and mastered will become secondary to human relations skills when you begin managing people. As you acquire more and more managerial responsibilities, your technical skills become less and less important, and give way to human relations skills and conceptual (decision making) skills. All this suggests that most of us spend most of our formal education studying something that will become less and less important to us as we progress through our managerial careers. So, although it is not possible to become "vice-president of organizational behaviour", the concepts you study will be relevant throughout your managerial career.

SYSTEMS APPROACH TO THE STUDY OF ORGANIZATION BEHAVIOUR

There is a wide agreement among organizational theorists that a system perspective offers important insights in the workings of an organization. The idea of systems is introduced and the difference between open and closed systems is discussed. It will demonstrate how the open systems approach can help us conceptualize better what is that organizations do.

A system is defined as a set of interrelated and interdependent parts arranged in a manner that produces a unified whole. Societies are systems, and so as plants and human bodies. They take inputs, transform them and produce some output. The unique characteristic of the systems viewpoint is the interrelationship of parts within the system. Every system is characterized by two diverse forces—differentiation and integration. In a system, specialized functions are differentiated, which replace diffuse global patterns. In the human body, the lungs, the heart and the liver are all distinct functions. Similarly, organizations have divisions, departments, and like units separated out to perform specialized activities. At the same time, in order to maintain unity among the differential parts and form a complete whole, every system has a reciprocal process of integration. In organization, this integration is typically achieved through devices such as coordinated levels of hierarchy; direct supervision; and rules, procedures, and policies. Every system, therefore, requires differentiation to identify its subjects and integration to ensure that this system doesn't break down into separate elements.

Although organizations are made up of parts or systems, they are themselves subsystems within larger systems. There are not only systems but there are subsystems and suprasystems. The classification of these three depends on the unit of analysis. "X" College is a subsystem within "B" University system. If we focus our attention on "B" University as a system, then we also recognize that it functions as parts of the larger suprasystem of the Ministry of Education.

TYPES OF SYSTEMS

Systems are classified as either closed or open.

Closed System

It views the system as self-contained. Its dominant characteristic is that it essentially ignores the effect of the environment on the system. A perfect closed system would be one that receives no energy from an outside source and from which no energy is released to its surroundings. More idealistic than practical, the closed system perspective has little applicability to the study of organizations.

Open System

The open system recognizes the dynamic interaction of the system with its environment. Figure 2.1 depicts a simplified graphic representation of the open system. It is not difficult for us not to view organizations as closed system.

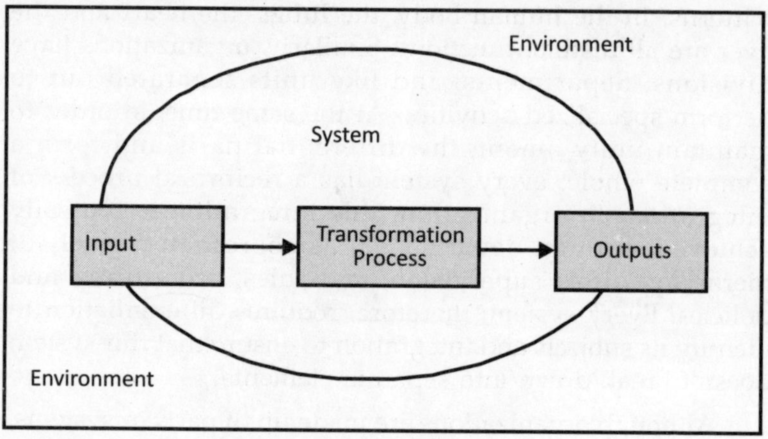

Fig. 2.1: **Basic Open System**

Source: Robbins, Stephan P., *Organization Theory, Structure, Design and Applications*. Prentice-Hall of India Private Limited, 1990, p. 13, New Delhi, India.

Organizations obtain their raw materials and human resources from the environment. They further depend on clients and customers in the environment to absorb their output. Banks take in deposits, convert these deposits into loans and other investments, and use the resulting profits to maintain themselves, to grow, and to pay dividends and taxes. The bank system, therefore, interacts actively with its environment, which is made up of people with savings to invest, other people in need of loans, potential employees looking for work, regulatory agencies, and the like. Figure 2.2 provides a more complex picture of an open system, as it would apply to an industrial organization. We see inputs of materials, labour, and capital. We see a technological process created for transforming raw materials in to finished product. The finished product, in turn, is sold to a customer. Financial institutions, the labour force, suppliers, and customers are all part of the environment, as is government.

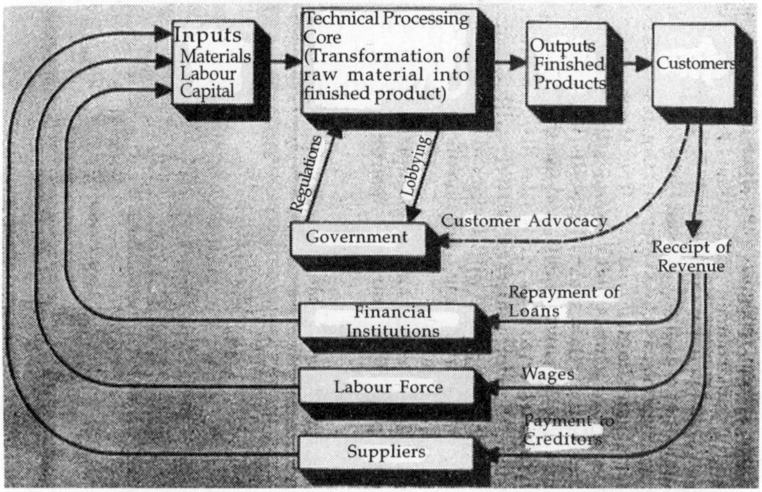

Fig. 2.2: **An Industrial Organization as an Open System**

Source: Robbins, Stephan P., *Organization Theory, Structure, Design and Applications*. Prentice-Hall of India Private Limited, 1990, p. 14, New Delhi, India.

All systems must have some interaction with their environments if they are to survive. Probably the most relevant way in which to look at the closed-open dichotomy is to consider it as a range rather than as two clearly separate classifications. In this way, we can explain that the degree to which a system is opened or closed varies within systems. An open system, for instance, may become more closed if contact with the environment is reduced over time. The reverse would also be true.

Characteristics of an Open System

All systems have inputs, transformation processes, and outputs. They take things such as raw materials, energy, information, and human resources and convert them in to goods and services, profits, waste materials, and the like. Open systems, however, have some additional characteristics that have relevance to the study of organizations.

1. *Environment awareness*

   One of the most obvious characteristics of an open system is its recognition of the interdependency between the system and its environment. There is a boundary that separates it from the environment. Changes in the environment affect one or more attributes of the system, and conversely changes in the system affect environment. Without a boundary there is no system, and the boundary or boundaries determine where the system and the sub-systems start and stop. Boundaries can be physical, like the clear lines that separate Ethiopia from its neighbors to the east and west, north and south. At this point, it is sufficient to acknowledge that the concept of boundaries is required for an understanding of systems and that their demarcation for the study of organization is problematic.

2. *Feedback*

   Open systems continually receive information from their environment. This helps the system to adjust and allows it to take corrective action to rectify deviations from its prescribed course. This receipt of environmental information is called feedback; that is a process that allows a portion of the output to be returned to the system as input (such as information or money) so as to modify succeeding outputs from the system.

3. *Cyclical character*

   Open system are cycles of events. The systems output furnish the means for new inputs that allow for the repetition of the cycle. For instance, the revenue received from the customers by the industrial firm must be adequate enough to pay creditors and the wages of employees and to repay loans if the life cycle is to be perpetuated and the survival of the organization maintained.

4. *Negative entropy*

   The term entropy refers to the propensity of a system to run down or disintegrate. A closed system, because it does not import energy or new inputs from its environment, will run down over time. In contrast an open system is characterized by negative entropy— it can repair itself, maintain its structure, avoid death, and even grow because it has the ability to import more energy than it puts out.

5. *Steady state*

   The input of energy to arrest entropy maintains some constancy in energy exchange resulting in relatively a steady state. Even though there is a constant flow of new inputs into the system and a steady outflow, on balance the character of the system remains the same. Our body will replace most of its dying cells, but our physical appearance alters very little. So while an open system is active in processing inputs to outputs, the system tends to maintain itself over time.

6. *Movement toward growth and expansion*

   The steady state characteristic is descriptive and of simple or primitive open systems. As the system becomes more complex and moves to counteract entropy, open systems move toward growth and expansion. This is not a contradiction of the steady-state thesis. To ensure their survival large and complex systems operate in a way to acquire some margin of safety beyond the immediate level of existence. The many sub-systems within the system, to avoid entropy tend to import more energy than is required for its output. The result is that the steady state is applicable to simple systems but, at more complex levels, becomes one of preserving the character of the system through growth and expansion. Remember that the basic system does not change directly as a result of expansion. The most growth pattern is one in which there is merely a multiplication of the same type of cycles or subsystems. The quantity of the system changes while the quality remains the same.

7. *Balance of maintenance and adaptive activities*
Open systems seek to reconcile two, often conflicting, activities called maintenance activities and adaptive activities. Maintenance activities ensure that the various sub-systems are in balance and the total system is in accord with its environment. This, in effect, prevents rapid changes that may unbalance the system. In contrast, adaptive activities are necessary so that the system can adjust over time to variations to internal and external demands. Both maintenance and adaptive activities are required if a system is to survive. Stable and well-maintained organizations that do not adapt as conditions change, will not endure long. Similarly the adaptive and unstable organization will be inefficient and unlikely to survive for long.
8. *Equifinality*
The concept of equifinality states that a system can reach a final state from differing initial conditions and by a variety of paths. This means that an organizational system can accomplish its objectives with varied inputs and transformation processes.

The importance of the system perspective lies in:

1. Encouraging all managers to identify and understand the environment in which the system operates.
2. Helping managers to see the organization as a stable patterns and actions within boundaries and to gain insights into why organizations are resistant to change.
3. Directing managers' attention to alternative inputs and processes for reaching their goals.

The system's framework has its own limitations, the most telling being its abstractness. Its value lies more in conceptual framework than its direct applicability to solving managers' organizational problems.

HAWTHORNE STUDIES

A major step on the way to current organizational behaviour theory was the human relations movement that began in the 1930s and continued in various forms until the 1950s. Popularized by Elton Mayo and his famous Hawthorne studies conducted at the Hawthorne plant of the Western Electric Company, in many ways it remains the foundation of much of our management thinking today. The initial experiments reflected strongly the physical orientation of scientific management, since they were designed to explore the relationship between lighting and productivity. The rational approach of scientific management predicted a positive relationship; i.e., as lighting increased, productivity would increase — up to a point, of course. Logically, at some (high) level of illumination, productivity should begin to decline, so the original experiment was designed to determine the optimal level of illumination. However, the researchers found no predictable relationship between lighting and output and because the research results could not be explained by existing knowledge, the researchers were forced to find new explanations. Further research indicated that the lack of a predictable relationship between lighting and output was related to the mental and emotional side of organizations rather than the physical and mechanistic side, recognized by scientific management. Additional studies showed that economic factors, such as incentive systems, were equally poor in predicting behaviour.

It should be noted that the physical variables studied included such things as illumination, rest periods, length of work periods, and length of work week — all in an attempt to find the optimal level of each. But as the experiments continued, non-physical variables were also studied, such as improved human relations, supervisory methods, social interactions, incentive systems, and worker autonomy. In general, the researchers concluded that social factors were more important determinants of employee behaviour and productivity than physical and economic factors. Something called "morale" was suggested as being related to productivity and morale was found to be related to factors such as style of supervision, personal relationships on the job, freedom to choose work methods, and a concept called "group norms". The recognition of the importance of these factors opened up much opportunity for advances in the theory and practice of management.

The human relations movement, like scientific management, is not without its shortcomings. Because of the nature of its findings and the resulting lessons for managers, it has been criticized as "cow sociology" (so-called because happy cows presumably give more milk). This simplistic view of the relationship between morale and productivity is something that existing research has not been able to verify. The view has also caused misconceptions about what "correct" management methods are. A common interpretation of the human relations movement is that managers need only treat their employees well to generate maximum productivity. This conclusion is unfortunate for two reasons. First, as the material in subsequent chapters will show, it is oversimplified and therefore often inaccurate. Second, those who do not agree with this conclusion might be labeled advocates of poor treatment of employees — which, of course, is also false. Quite possibly, the positive but simplistic philosophy of human relations has actually hindered needed research into organizational behaviour.

Hawthorne Legacy

In recent years attempts have been made to reexamine the Hawthorne experiments in light of new research regarding the relationship between morale and productivity. Interviews conducted decades later with three subjects of the Hawthorne studies and reanalysis of the original data with modern statistical techniques do not support initial conclusions about the positive effect of supportive supervision. Specifically, money, fear of unemployment during the great depression, managerial discipline, and high quality raw materials—not supportive supervision—turned out to be responsible for high output in the relay assembly test room experiments. Nonetheless, the human relations movement gathered momentum through the 1950s, as academics and managers alike made stirring claims about the powerful effect that individual needs, supportive supervision, and group dynamics apparently had on job performance.

AGE OF HUMAN AND SOCIAL CAPITAL

Management is a lot like juggling. Everything is constantly in motion, with several things up in the air at any given time. Strategically speaking, managers juggle human, financial, material, informational, and technological resources. Each is vital to success in its own way. But jugglers remind us that some objects are rubber and some are glass. Dropped rubber objects bounce; dropped glass objects break. As more and more managers have come to realize, we cannot afford to drop the people factor.

Human capital is the productive potential of an individual's knowledge and actions. Potential is the operative word in this intentionally broad definition. When you are hungry, money in your pocket is good because it has the potential to buy a meal. Likewise, a present or future employee with the right combination of knowledge, skills, and motivation to excel represents human capital with the potential to give the organization a competitive advantage.

What is social capital? Our focus now shifts from the individual to social units (e.g. friends, family, company, group or club, nation). Think relationships. Social capital is productive potential resulting from strong relationships, goodwill, trust, and cooperative effort. Again, the word potential is key. According to experts on the subject: "it's true: the social capital that used to be a given in organizations is now rare and endangered. But the social capital we can build will allow us to capitalize on the volatile, virtual possibilities of today's business environment".

Summary

- Organizational behaviour, commonly referred to as OB, is an interdisciplinary field dedicated to better understanding and managing people at work.

- A major step on the way to current organizational behaviour theory was the human relations movement that began in the 1930s and continued in various forms until the 1950s
- Human capital is the productive potential of an individual's knowledge and actions. Social capital is productive potential resulting from strong relationships, goodwill, trust, and cooperative effort.

Self-Learning Activity

Try to answer the following questions on your own:

1. Explain the nature and scope of OB.
2. Describe Hawthorne Experiments.
3. What do you understand about Human and social capital?

3

Basic Psychological Process

Individual differences: Self-concept, Personality and Emotions

Self-Concept

Self is the core of one's conscious existence. Awareness of self is referred to as one's self-concept. Sociologist Viktor Gecas defines self-concept as "The concept the individual has himself as a physical, social and spiritual or moral being". Because you have a self-concept, you recognize yourself as a distinct human being. A self-concept would be impossible without the capacity to think. This brings us the capacity to think. This brings us to the role of cognitions.

Cognitions represent "any knowledge, opinion, or belief about the environment, about oneself, or about one's behaviour". There are many different types of cognitions; the following are relevant to organizational behaviour. Anticipation, planning, goal setting, evaluating, and setting personal standards Ideas of self and self-concept vary from one historical era to another, one socio-economic class to another, and culture to culture.

Self-Esteem

Self-esteem is a belief about one's own self-worth based on the overall self-evaluation. There are:

- People with high self-esteem view themselves in positive terms:

- Those who agree with positive statements and disagree with negative statements have high self-esteem.
- They see themselves as worthwhile, capable and acceptable.

❖ People with low self-esteem view themselves in negative terms. They do not feel good about themselves and are hampered by self-doubts.

Self-Efficacy

Self-efficacy is a person's belief about his or her chances of successfully accomplishing a specific task. According to one organizational behaviour (OB) writer:

> "Self-efficacy arises from the gradual acquisition of complex cognitive, social, linguistic, and/or physical skills through experience".

Childhood experiences have a powerful effect on a person's self-efficacy. Efficacy-performance cycles can spiral upward toward success or downward toward failure.

NB

❖ People with high self-efficacy expectations tend to have high success rates.

❖ Whereas people with low self-efficacy expectations tend to have low success rates.

❖ Chronically low self-efficacy is associated with a condition called learned helplessness—the severely debilitating belief that one has no control over one's environment.

Self-Monitoring

Self-monitoring is the extent to which a person observes their own self-expressive behaviour and adapts it to the demands of the situation.

❖ There are high self-monitors and low self-monitors in organizational life.

❖ Both high and low self-monitors are subject to criticism.

- High self-monitors are sometimes called chameleons who readily adapt their self presentation to their surroundings.
- Low self-monitors often are criticized for being on their own planet and insensitive to others.

Within an OB context self-monitoring:

- is like any other individual difference — not a matter of right or wrong or good versus bad;
- but rather a source of diversity that needs to be adequately understood by present and future managers.

Organizational Identification

Organizational identification: a social aspect of self-concept with ethical implications

- Organizational values or beliefs become part of one's identity.
- When an employee comes to define him or herself with a specific organization, a psychological process— called organizational identification—happens.
- Organizational identification occurs when one comes to integrate beliefs about one's organization into one's identity.
- Organizational identification goes to the heart of organizational culture and socialization.

With the express intent of integrating the organization/ company into each employee's self-identity, managers put emphasis on Organizational mission, Organizational philosophy, and Organizational values.

Employees who identity closely with the organization will be more loyal, more committed and harder working.

Personality: Concepts and Controversy

Individuals have their own way of thinking and acting, their own unique style or personality.

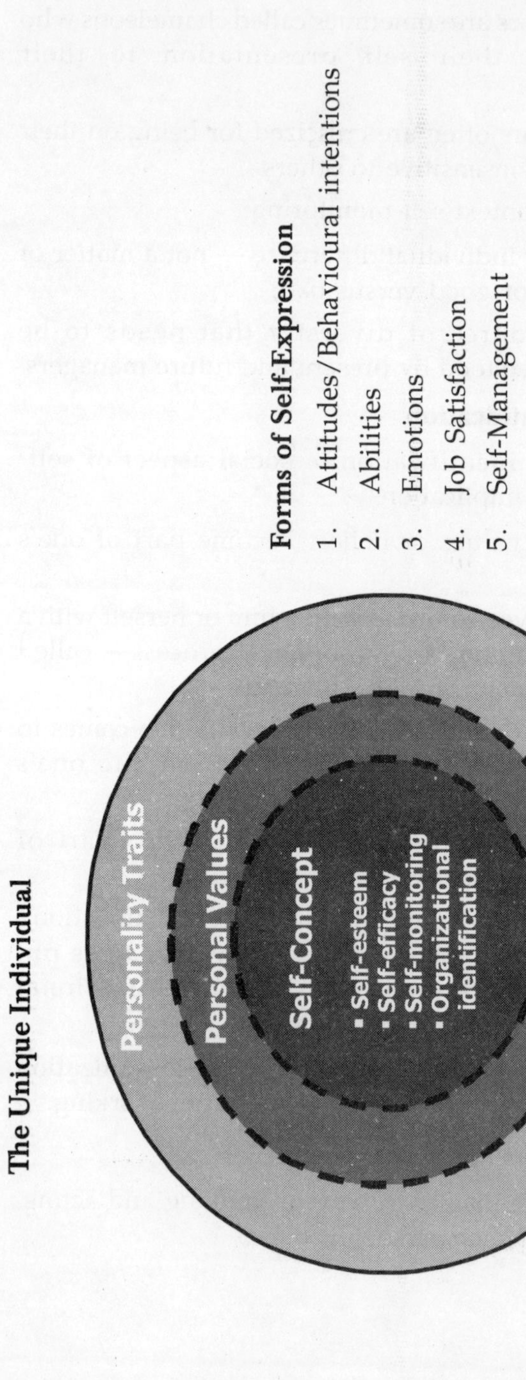

Fig. 3.1: **Instructional Road Map of Individual Differences in OB**

- Personality is defined as the combination of stable physical and mental characteristics that give the individual his or her identity.
- These characteristics or traits — including how one looks, thinks, acts, and feels — are the product of interacting genetic and environmental influences.

Five Personality Dimensions

The big five personality dimensions include: Extraversion, Agreeableness, Conscientiousness, Emotional stability, and Openness to experience (Table 3.1 for descriptions). A person's scores on the big five reveal a personality profile as unique as his or her fingerprints.

Table 3.1: The Big Five Personality Dimensions

Personality Dimension	Characteristics of a Person Scoring Positively on the Dimension
1. Extraversion	Outgoing, talkative, social, assertive
2. Agreeableness	Trusting, good natured, cooperative, soft hearted
3. Conscientiousness	Dependable, responsible, achievement, oriented, persistent
4. Emotional stability	Relaxed, secure, unworried
5. Openness to experience	Intellectual, imaginative, curious, broad minded

Those interested in OB want to know the connection between the big five and job performance.

The big five personality dimensions that correlate positively and strongly with job performance would be helpful in the selection, training, and appraisal of employees.

Proactive Personality

Someone who scores high on the big five dimension of conscientiousness is probably a good worker. Proactive personality is action-oriented person who shows initiative and perseveres to change things. Thomas S. Bateman and J. Michael Crant define and characterize the proactive personality in these terms: "someone who is relatively unconstrained by situational forces and who effects environmental change".

- Proactive people identify opportunities and act on them, show initiative, take action, and persevere until meaningful change occurs.

In short, people with proactive personalities are "hardwired" to change the status quo.

Positive and Negative Emotions

Richard S. Lazarus defines emotions as "complex, patterned, organismic reactions to how we think we are doing in our lifelong efforts to survive and flourish and to achieve what we wish for ourselves". The word organismic is appropriate because emotions involve the whole person—biological, psychological, and social. Psychologists draw a distinction between felt and displayed emotions. For example:

- *Felt emotion*—A person might feel angry at a rude co-worker
- *Displayed emotion*—A person might feel angry at a rude co-worker but not make a nasty remark in return.
- Emotions play roles in both causing and adapting to stress and its associated biological and psychological problems.

Lazarus's definition of emotions centers on a person's goals i.e., are goal-oriented. Lazarus identifies between:

- *Positive emotions:* The emotions you would experience are positive if they are congruent (or consistent) with an important lifetime goal. For example happiness/joy, Pride, Love/affection and Relief.
- *Negative emotions:* These are triggered by frustration and failure when pursuing one's goals. They are said to be goal incongruent.

It is important to note that the individual's goals may or may not be socially acceptable. Thus:

- A positive emotion, such as love/affection, may be undesirable if associated with sexual harassment.
- Oppositely, slight pangs of guilt, anxiety, and envy can motivate extra effort.
- On balance, the constructive or destructive nature of a particular emotion must be judged in terms of both its intensity and the person's relevant goal.

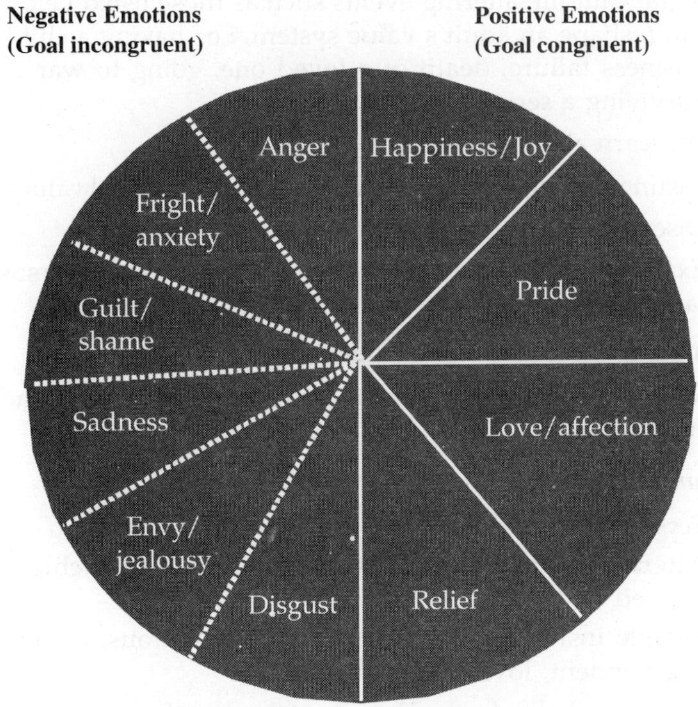

Fig. 3.2: **Positive and Negative Emotions**

Values, Attitudes, Abilities and Job Satisfaction

Personal Values

Values are defined as desired ways of behaving or desired end-states.

Value system - the organization one's beliefs about preferred way of behaving and desired end-states.

Researcher Milton Rokeach defined:

- A person's value system as an "enduring organization of beliefs concerning preferable modes of conduct or end-states of existence along a continuum of relative importance.
- Lifelong behaviour patterns are dictated by values that are set by the time people are in their early teens.
- Significant life-altering events such as those listed below can reshape an adult's value system, i.e., having a child, business failure, death of a loved one, going to war or Surviving a serious accident or disease.

We learn about personal values by:

- Distinguishing between instrumental and terminal values;
- Discussing three types of value conflict; and
- Examining the timely value-related topic of work versus family life conflicts.

Instrumental and Terminal Values

Rokeach distinguished between instrumental values and terminal values.

Instrumental Values

- Personally preferred ways of behaving
- Alternative behaviours/means by which we achieve desired ends.
- Sample instrumental values include ambitious, honest, independent, loving and obedient.

Someone who ranks the instrumental value "honest" highly, relative to the other instrumental values, is likely to be more honest than someone who gives it a low ranking.

Terminal Values

- Personally preferred end-states existence.
- Highly ranked terminal values include—A sense of accomplishment, happiness, pleasure, salvation and wisdom.

A sense of accomplishment, happiness, pleasure, salvation, and wisdom are: desired end-states or life goals.

Some would say terminal values are what life is all about. History is full of examples of people who were persecuted or put to death for their passionately held terminal values.

Value Conflicts

There are three types of value conflict of which we must be aware. Knowing how to recognize and deal effectively with them are major quality-of-life issues. They are:

1. Intrapersonal (inside the person) value conflict.
2. Interpersonal (between people) value conflict.
3. Individual-organization (between the person and the organization) value conflict.

Intrapersonal Value Conflict

(a) Inner conflict and resultant stress are experienced when 'highly ranked instrumental and terminal values' pull the individual in different directions.

(b) This is somewhat akin to role conflict.

(c) The main difference is influence:

  (i) Role conflict involves outside social expectations;

  (ii) Intrapersonal value conflict involves internal priorities.

Interpersonal Value Conflict

1. This type of value conflict often is at the core of personality conflicts.
2. People have different styles that may or may not mesh.
3. They embrace 'unique combinations of instrumental and terminal values' that inevitably spark disagreement.

Individual-organization Value Conflict

Organizations/companies actively seek to embed certain values into their corporate cultures. Conflict can occur when values espoused and enacted by the organization collide with employees' personal values. This is a common and persistent problem.

Attitudes

- Managers conduct attitude surveys to monitor such things as job and pay satisfaction in the workplace.
- Attention to attitudes is based on the assumption that attitudes somehow influence behaviour such as voting for someone, working hard or quitting one's job. In the following section we examine the connection between attitudes and behaviour; and explore the important work attitudes of job satisfaction, organizational commitment, and job involvement.

Nature of Attitudes

An attitude is defined as "a learned predisposition to respond in a consistently favorable or unfavorable manner with respect to a given object". Attitudes affect behaviour at a different level than do values. Values represent global beliefs that influence behaviour across all situations. Attitudes relate only to behaviour directed toward specific objects, persons, or situations. Values and attitudes generally, but not always, are in harmony. A manager who strongly values helpful behaviour may have a negative attitude toward helping an unethical co-worker. The difference between attitudes and values is clarified by considering the three components of attitudes: Affective, Cognitive and Behavioural.

Affective Component

The affective component of an attitude contains the feelings or emotions one has about a given object or situation. How do you feel about people who talk on cell/mobile phones in restaurants? Two opposite possible feelings:

1. *A feeling of annoys or anger* - You are expressing negative affect or feelings toward people who talk on cell phones in restaurants.
2. *Neutral feeling* - You are indifferent about people talking on cell phones in restaurants.

Cognitive Component

Cognitive component is the beliefs or ideas one has about on object or situation.

What do you think about people who talk on cell phones in restaurants?

Do you believe this behaviour is inconsiderate, productive, completely acceptable or rude. The answer you give represents the cognitive component of your attitude toward people talking on cell phones in restaurants.

Behavioural Component

- It refers to how one intends to act toward someone or something.
- For example, how would you intend to respond to someone talking on a cell phone during dinner at a restaurant if this individual were sitting in close proximity to you and your guest?
- Attitude theory suggests that your ultimate behaviour in this situation is a function of all three attitudinal components:
  - You are unlikely to say anything to someone using a cell phone in a restaurant if you are not irritated by this behaviour (affective).
  - If you believe cell phone use helps people to manage their lives (cognitive).
  - If you have no intention of confronting this individual (behavioural).

Key Work Attitudes

- Attitudes toward work have changed throughout the recorded history.
- People have a multitude of attitudes about things that happen to them at work, but OB researchers have focused on a limited number of them.
- We will examine three work attitudes that have important practical implications:
  - Job satisfaction.
  - Organizational commitment.
  - Job involvement.

Job Satisfaction

- ❖ Reflects the extent to which an individual likes his or her job.
- ❖ It may be defined as affective or emotional response toward various facets of one's job.

This definition implies that job satisfaction is not a unitary concept i.e., a person can be relatively satisfied with one aspect of his or her job and dissatisfied with one or more other aspects.

Organizational Commitment

- ❖ Reflects the extent to which an individual identifies with an organization and is committed to its goals.
- ❖ It is an important work attitude because committed individuals are expected to display:
  - A willingness to work harder to achieve organizational goals; and
  - A greater desire to stay employed at an organization.

Job Involvement

Job involvement is defined as:

- ❖ "The degree to which one is cognitively preoccupied with, engaged in, and concerned with one's present job".
- ❖ This work attitude manifests itself through the extent to which people are immersed in their job tasks.

Abilities and Performance

Ability — stable characteristic responsible for a person's maximum physical or mental performance.

- ❖ Individual differences in abilities and accompanying skills are a central concern for managers because nothing can be accomplished without appropriately skilled personnel.
- ❖ Ability represents a broad and stable characteristic responsible for a person's maximum — as opposed to typical — performance on mental and physical tasks.
- ❖ A skill — is the specific capacity to physically manipulate objects.

- Consider this difference as you imagine yourself being the only passenger on a small commuter airplane in which the pilot has just passed out. As the plane nose dives, your effort and abilities will not be enough to save yourself and the pilot if you do not possess flying skills.
- Successful performance depends on the right combination of effort, ability and skill.

Intelligence and Cognitive Abilities

Intelligence

- Represents an individual's capacity for constructive thinking, reasoning, and problem solving.
- Intelligence was believed to be an innate capacity passed genetically from one generation to the next.
- Research since has sown that intelligence (like personality) also is a function of environmental influences.

Types of Abilities

Charles Spearman (1927) proposed that all cognitive performance is determined by two types of abilities.

1. A general mental ability needed for all cognitive tasks.
2. Unique ability to the task at hand.

For example an individual's ability to complete crossword puzzles is a function of his or her broad mental abilities as well as the specific ability to perceive patterns in partially completed words. One research psychologist listed 120 distinct mental abilities. Seven major mental abilities are the most frequently cited mental abilities (Table 3.2). Of the seven abilities, personnel selection researchers have found the following to be valid predictors of job performance for both minority and majority applicants. Verbal ability, Numerical ability, Spatial ability, and Inductive reasoning.

Table 3.2: Mental abilities underlying performance

Abilities	Description
1. Verbal comprehension	The ability to understand what words mean and to readily comprehend what is read.
2. Word fluency	The ability to produce isolated words that fulfill specific symbolic or structural requirements (such as all words that begin with the letter b and have two vowels).
3. Numerical	The ability to make quick and accurate arithmetic computations such as adding and subtracting.
4. Spatial	Being able to perceive spatial patterns and to visualize how geometric shapes would look if transformed in shape or position.
5. Memory	Having good rote memory for paired words, symbols, lists of numbers, or other associated items.
6. Perceptual speed	The ability to perceive figures, identify similarities and differences, and carry out tasks involving visual perception.
7. Inductive reasoning	The ability to reason from specifics to general conclusions.

Causes and Consequences of Job Satisfaction

Causes of Job Satisfaction

Five predominant models of job satisfaction focus on different causes. They are— need fulfillment, discrepancy, value attainment, equity, and dispositional/genetic components. A brief review of these models will provide insight into the complexity of this seemingly simple concept.

1. *Need fulfillment*

These models propose that satisfaction is determined by the extent to which the characteristics of a job allow an individual to fulfill his or her needs.

2. *Discrepancies*

These models propose that satisfaction is a result of met expectations.

- Met expectations represent the difference between what an individual expects to receive from a job, such as good pay and promotional opportunities, and what he or she actually receives.
    - When expectations are greater than what is received, a person will be dissatisfied.
    - In contrast, this model predicts the individual will be satisfied when he or she attains outcomes above and beyond expectations.

3. *Value attainment*

The idea underlying value attainment is that satisfaction results from the perception that a job allows for fulfillment of an individual's important work values:

- In general value fulfillment is positively related to job satisfaction.
- Managers can thus enhance employee satisfaction by structuring the work environment and its associated rewards and recognition to reinforce employees' values.

4. *Equity*

In this model, satisfaction is a function of how "fairly" an individual is treated at work.

- Satisfaction results from one's perception that work outcomes, relative to inputs, compare favorably with a significant other's outcomes/inputs.
- Employees' perceptions of being treated fairly at work were highly related to overall job satisfaction.
- Managers are encouraged to monitor employees' fairness perceptions and to interact with employees in such a way that they feel equitably treated.

5. *Dispositional/genetic components*

This model is based on the belief that job satisfaction is partly a function of both personal traits and genetic factors.

This model implies that stable individual differences are just as important in explaining job satisfaction, as are characteristics of the work environment. Studies support a positive, significant relationship between personal traits and job satisfaction (over time periods ranging from 2 to 50 years). Genetic factors also were found to significantly predict life satisfaction well-being, and general job satisfaction. Overall, researchers estimate that 30 per cent of an individual's job satisfaction is associated with dispositional and genetic components.

Major Correlates and Consequences of Job Satisfaction

This area has significant managerial implications. Because thousands of studies have examined the relationship between job satisfaction and other organizational variables. We will consider the more important variables from the standpoint of managerial relevance (Table 3.3). The relationship between job satisfaction and these other variables is either positive or negative. The strength of the relationship ranges from weak (very little relationship) to strong. Strong relationships imply that managers can significantly influence the variable of interest by increasing job satisfaction.

Table 3.3: Correlation of job satisfaction

Variables Related with Satisfaction	Direction of Relationship	Strength of Relationship
Motivation	Positive	Moderate
Organizational citizenship behaviour	Positive	Moderate
Absenteeism	Negative	Weak
Tardiness	Negative	Weak
Withdrawal cognitions	Negative	Strong
Turnover	Negative	Moderate
Heart disease	Negative	Moderate
Perceived stress	Negative	Strong
Pro-union voting	Negative	Moderate
Job performance	Positive	Moderate
Life satisfaction	Positive	Moderate
Mental health	Positive	Moderate

Source: Kreitner R., and Kinicki A., *Organizational Behaviour*, McGraw - Hill, 2004, USA, p. 213.

Seven Key Correlates of Job Satisfaction

Motivation

Studies reveal a significant positive relationship between motivation and job satisfaction.

- ❖ Because satisfaction with supervision also was significantly correlated with motivation managers are advised to consider how their behaviour affects employee satisfaction.
- ❖ Managers can potentially enhance employees' motivation through various attempts to increase job satisfaction.

Organizational Citizenship Behaviour (OCBs)

OCBs consist of employee behaviours that are beyond the call of duty. Examples include:

- Constructive statements about the department.
- Expression of personal interest in the work of others.
- Suggestions for improvement.
- Training new people.
- Respect for the spirit as well as the letter of housekeeping rules.
- Care for organizational property.
- Punctuality and attendance well beyond standard or enforceable levels.

Managers certainly would like employees to exhibit these behaviours.

Studies revealed a significant and moderately positive correlation between organizational citizenship behaviours and job satisfaction, demonstrated that employees' citizenship behaviours were determined more by leadership and characteristics of the work environment than by an employee's personality. It appears that managerial behaviour significantly influences an employee's willingness to exhibit citizenship behaviours.

Absenteeism

Absenteeism is costly, and managers are constantly on the lookout for ways to reduce it by increasing job satisfaction.

- ❖ There should be a strong negative relationship (or negative correlation) between satisfaction and absenteeism.
- ❖ As satisfaction increases, absenteeism should decrease.
- ❖ Research results revealed a weak negative relationship between satisfaction and absenteeism.
- ❖ It is unlikely that managers will realize any significant decrease in absenteeism by increasing job satisfaction.

Withdrawal Cognitions

Withdrawal cognitions are overall thoughts and feelings about quitting a job. Some people quit their jobs impulsively or in a fit of anger. Most go through a process of thinking about whether or not they should quit. What causes an individual to think about quitting his or her job? Job satisfaction is believed to be one of the most significant contributors.

Turnover

Turnover disrupts organizational continuity and is very costly. For example, increases the direct costs of recruiting and training new employees; and increases the indirect costs associated with impaired service quality, lost business to competitors, loss of technical knowledge and human capital, and decreased morale and increased turnover among remaining workers.

Although there are many different things a manager can do to reduce employee turnover, many of them revolve around attempts to improve employees' job satisfaction. Studies reveal that job satisfaction obtained a moderate negative relationship with employee turnover. Given this relationship, managers are advised to try to reduce employee turnover by increasing employee job satisfaction.

Perceived Stress

Stress can have very negative effects on organizational behaviour and an individual's health.

Stress is positively related to Absenteeism, turnover, coronary heart disease and viral infections. Studies reveal that perceived stress has a strong negative relationship with job satisfaction. It is hoped that managers would attempt to reduce the negative effects of stress by improving job satisfaction.

Job Performance

Job performance one of the biggest controversies within OB research centers on the relationship between job satisfaction and job performance. The dominant beliefs are either that satisfaction causes performance or performance causes satisfaction.

To resolve this controversy a team of researchers recently attempted and reached at two key findings:

1. Job satisfaction and performance are moderately related. This is an important finding because it supports the belief that employee job satisfaction is a key work attitude managers should consider when attempting to increase employees' job performance.
2. The relationship between job satisfaction and performance is much more complex than originally thought.

It is not as simple as satisfaction causing performance or performance causing satisfaction. Researchers now believe both variables indirectly influence each other through a host of individual differences and work-environment characteristics.

Social perception and attributions An information processing model of perception

❖ Perception is a cognitive process that enables us to interpret and understand our surroundings.

❖ Recognition of objects is one of this process's major functions. For example:

- Both people and animals recognize familiar objects in their environments.

❖ People must recognize objects to meaningfully interact with their environment.

❖ Since OB's principal focus is on people the emphasis given on social perception rather than object perception.

Four-Stage sequence and a working example

❖ Perception involves a four stage information processing sequence.

❖ Three of the stages are:
- Selective attention/Comprehension;
- Encoding and simplification; and
- Storage and retention.

The three stages describe how specific information and environmental stimuli are observed and stored in memory.

❖ The fourth stage i.e. retrieval and response, involves turning mental representations into real world judgments and decisions.

Stage 1: Selective attention/comprehension

❖ People are constantly bombarded by physical and social stimuli in the environment.

❖ They do not have the mental capacity to fully comprehend all this information.

❖ They selectively perceive subsets of environmental stimuli.

❖ Attention plays a role.
- Attention is the process of becoming consciously aware of something or someone.

❖ Attention can be focused on information either from
- the environment or
- Memory.

- Regarding attention from memory, if you find yourself thinking about totally unrelated events or people while reading a textbook, your memory is the focus of your attention.
- Research has shown that people tend to pay attention to salient stimuli.

Salient stimuli — something is salient when it stands out from its context. For example:

- A 250-pound man would certainly be salient in a women's aerobics class.
- But not at a meeting of the national football league players' association.

Salience is determined by several factors, including:

- Being novel (the only person in a group of that race, gender, hair colour, or age)
- Being bright (wearing a yellow shirt)
- Being unusual for a person's social category (such as a university president driving a motorcycle to work).

Stage 2: Encoding and simplification

Observed information is not stored in memory in its original form.

- Encoding is required; raw information is interpreted or translated into mental representations.
- To accomplish this, perceivers assign pieces of information to cognitive categories.
- "By category we mean a number of objects that are considered equivalent. Categories are generally designated by names, for example,
    - Dog, animal
    - People
    - Events and objects

Are interpreted and evaluated by comparing their characteristics with information contained in schemata.

Schemata: A schema represents a person's mental picture or summary of a particular event or type of stimulus. *Schema: mental picture of an event or object*.

Cognitive: Category labels are needed to make schemata meaningful. Cognitive categories: mental depositories for storing information.

Encoding outcomes

- ❖ We use the encoding process to interpret and evaluate our environment.
- ❖ This process can result in differing interpretations and evaluations of the same person or event.
- ❖ Varying interpretations of what we observe occur due to four key reasons.
  1. People possess different information in the schemata used for interpretation
     - *(a)* Women and men had different opinions on sexual harassment. Women defined a broader range of behaviours as harassing.
  2. Our moods and emotions influence our focus of attention and evaluations of others.
  3. People tend to apply recently used cognitive categories during encoding.
  4. Individual differences influence encoding. Pessimistic or depressive individuals tend to interpret their surroundings more negatively than optimistic and happy people.

The point is that we should not be surprised when people interpret and evaluate the same situation or event differently.

Researchers are currently trying to identify the host of factors that influence the encoding process.

Stage 3: Storage and retention

This phase involves storage of information in long-term memory.

❖ Long-term memory is like an apartment complex consisting of separate units connected to one another.

❖ Long-term memory - consists of separate but related categories.

❖ The connected categories contain different types of information. Information also passes among these categories.

❖ Long-term memory is made up of three compartments (or wings) containing categories of information about:

- Events;
- Semantic materials; and
- People.

Event memory

❖ This compartment is composed of categories containing information about both specific and general events.

❖ These memories describe appropriate sequences of events in well-known situations, e.g. going to the college dining hall or going to the library etc.

Semantic memory

❖ Semantic memory refers to general knowledge about the world. In so doing, it functions as a mental dictionary of concepts. Each concept contains a definition, for example,

- (A good leader) and associated traits (outgoing);
- Emotional states (happy);
- Physical characteristics (tall); and
- Behaviours (works hard).

Just as there are schemata for general events, concepts in semantic memory are stored as schemata.

Person Memory

❖ Categories within this compartment contain information about a single individual:

- Your instructor or
- Groups of people (managers).

Stage 4: Retrieval and response

- People retrieve information from memory when they make judgments and decisions.
- Our ultimate judgments and decisions are either based on the process of
  - Drawing on;
  - Interpreting; and
  - Integrated categorical information stored in long-term memory or on retrieving a summary judgment that was already made.

Stereotypes: Perceptions about groups of people

- Perception does result in some predictable outcomes (beauty is in the eye of the beholder).
- Managers can make use of perceptual outcomes to help them interact more efficiently with employees.
- For example, Table 3.4 the common perceptual errors.
- These perceptual errors often distort the evaluation of job applicants and job performance; managers need to guard against them.

Table 3.4: Commonly found Perceptual Errors

Perceptual Error	Description
Halo	A rater forms an overall impression about an object and then uses that impression to bias ratings about the object.
Leniency	A personal characteristic that leads an individual to consistently evaluate other people or objects in an extremely positive fashion.
Recency effects	The tendency to remember recent information. If the information is negative, the person or object is evaluated negatively.
Contrast effects	The tendency to evaluate people or objects by comparing them with characteristics of recently observed people or objects.

- The most important and potentially harmful outcomes associated with person perception is Stereotypes.
  - "A stereotype is an individual's set of beliefs about the characteristics or attributes of a group" stereotype are not always negative. For example,
    - The belief that engineers are good at math is certainly part of a stereotype.
    - Stereotypes may or may not be accurate. Engineers may in fact be better at math than the general population.
  - In general, stereotypic characteristics are used to differentiate a particular group of people from other groups.

1. *Sex role stereotype*

A sex-role stereotype is the belief that differing trait and abilities make men and women particularly well suited to different roles.

The results on the sex-role stereotypes held by adults in USA revealed the majority of respondents viewed women as:

- More emotional;
- Affectionate;
- Talkative;
- Patient; and
- Creative than men.

Men, on the other hand, were perceived as:

- More aggressive;
- Courageous;
- Easy-going; and
- Ambitious than women.

Research demonstrates that men and women do not systematically differ as stated above.

Note: Remember these stereotypes still persist.

2. *Age stereotypes*

Age stereotypes reinforce age discrimination because of their negative orientation.

❖ For example, long- standing age stereotypes depict older workers as:

- Less satisfied;
- Not as involved with their work;
- Less motivated;
- Not as committed;
- less productive than their younger co-workers;
- More apt to be absent from work;
- Older employees are also perceived as being more accident prone.

Note: As with sex-role stereotypes, these stereotypes are based more on fiction than fact.

3. *Race stereotypes*

There are many different racial stereotypes that exist. For instance,

❖ African-Americans have been viewed as athletic and aggressive;

❖ Asians as quiet, introverted, smarter, and more quantitatively oriented; and

❖ Hispanics as family-oriented and religious.

Unfortunately, negative stereotypes such as some of those just listed are still apparent in many organizations.

4. *Disability stereotypes*

People with disabilities not only face negative stereotypes that affect their employability, but they also can be stigmatized by the general population.

Causal Attributions

Attribution theory is based on the premise that people attempt to infer causes for observe behaviour.

- ❖ Rightly or wrongly, we constantly formulate cause-and-effect explanations for our own and other's behaviour.
- ❖ Attributional statements such as the following are common: "Kebede drinks too much because he has no willpower; but I need a couple of drinks after work because I'm under a lot of pressure."
- ❖ Causal attributions are defined as *suspected or inferred causes of behaviour*.

NB: Even though our causal attributions tend to be self-serving and are often invalid, it is important to understand how people formulate attributions because they profoundly affect organizational behaviour. For example, a supervisor who attributes:

- ❖ An employee's poor performance to a lack of effort might reprimand that individual.
- ❖ Training might be deemed necessary if the supervisor attributes the poor performance to a lack of ability.

Attribution Tendencies

Researchers have uncovered two attribution tendencies that distort one's interpretation of observed behaviour:

1. Fundamental attribution bias; and
2. Self-serving bias.

Fundamental attribution bias: Ignoring environmental factors that affect behaviour.

- ❖ The fundamental attribution bias reflects one's tendency to attribute another person's behaviour to his or her personal characteristics, as opposed to situational factors.
- ❖ This bias causes perceivers to ignore important environmental forces that often significantly affect behaviour.

Self-serving bias: Taking more personal responsibility for success than failure.

- ❖ The self-serving bias
    - Represents one's tendency to take more personal responsibility for success than for failure.

- Suggests employees will attribute.
- Their success to internal factors (high ability or hard work).
- Their failures to uncontrollable external factors (tough job, bad luck, unproductive co-workers, or an unsympathetic boss).

Major Correlates and Consequences of Job Satisfaction

This area has significant managerial implications:

- ❖ Because thousands of studies have examined the relationship between job satisfaction and other organizational variables.
- ❖ We will consider the more important variables from the standpoint of managerial relevance.
- ❖ The relationship between job satisfaction and these other variables is either positive or negative.
- ❖ The strength of the relationship ranges from weak (very little relationship) to strong.
- ❖ Strong relationships imply that managers can significantly influence the variable of interest by increasing job satisfaction.
- ❖ Seven key correlates of job satisfaction.

Summary

- Awareness of self is referred to as one's self-concept.
- The big five personality dimensions include: Extraversion, Agreeableness, Conscientiousness, Emotional stability, and Openness to experience.

Self-Learning Activity

Try to answer the following questions on your own:

1. Discuss about value conflicts.
2. Write a note on Job satisfaction.
3. What do you understand from organizational citizenship behaviour?

4

Motivation

Definition

Shartle defines: "Motivation is a reported urge or tension to move in a given direction or to achieve a certain goal".

While the first management task is to set organisational goals, the major task is to move the organisation effectively, to reach that goal. This can be done by motivation, the purpose of which is to create a congenial climate as well as physical work environment. The central idea of motivation is the will to work. What ways and means could sharpen the will to work is the job of the motivator to find out. The managers must use relevant motivators for the efficient and achievement of the organisational objectives.

Edgar Schein, a psychologist viewed certain assumptions regarding man and motivation:

1. Man is primarily motivated by economic incentives and will do what gets him the greatest economic gain.
2. Since economic incentives are under the control of the organisation, man is essentially a passive agent to be manipulated, motivated and controlled by the organisation.
3. Man's feelings are essentially irrational and must be prevented from interfering with this rational calculation of self-interest.

4. Organisations can and must be designed in such a way as to neutralise and control man's feelings and therefore his unpredictable traits.

Elton Mayo, a behavioural scientist, gave the following assumptions on motivation:

1. Man is basically motivated by social needs and obtains his basic sense of identity through relationships with others.
2. As a result of the industrial revolution and the rationalisation of work, much of the meaning has gone out of work itself and must therefore be sought is the social relationships on the job.
3. Man is more responsive to the social forces of the peer group than to the incentives and controls of management.
4. Man is more responsive to management to the extent that a supervisor can meet a subordinate's needs and needs for acceptance.

Benefits of Motivation

1. Motivation provides a means of satisfying the needs of the subordinates.
2. It helps to boost the morale of the employees.
3. It increases productivity in the organisation.
4. It enhances the image of the organisation.
5. It fosters discipline among employees.
6. It creates a sense of responsibility at all levels of employees.
7. It encourages employees to dedicate and climb for higher positions.
8. It reduces tension and pave the way for cordial employer-employee relationship.

Some theories of motivation are discussed below:

1. *Abraham Maslow's Hierarchy of Needs*

This theory states that human needs have certain priority and arise in the form of hierarchy. He has put various needs into five levels ranging from the lowest order needs to the highest order needs having a definite sequence of domination. When one set of needs is satisfied, this kind of need ceases to be a motivator forcing a person to go for the next level of needs following the higher order needs. The five sets of needs from the lowest to the highest are given below in ascending order:

5. Self-actualisation needs
4. Esteem needs
3. Social needs
2. Safety needs
1. Psychological needs.

These needs are further explained as follows:

1. *Psychological Needs*

These are primarily the needs arising out of physiological or biological tension. The needs include the basic needs for food, water, shelter and sex.

2. *Safety Needs*

Safety and security needs are provisions against deprivation in the future. It also involves a sense of protection against danger and threats. In a civilized society, a person is usually protected from threats of violence, or extremes in climate or fear of material safety, hence, safety needs dwell on economic and job security, life and medical insurance and other protective measures to safeguard satisfaction of psychological needs in the future, which may be unpredictable.

3. *Love and Social Needs*

After the needs of the body and security are satisfied, then a sense of belonging and acceptance becomes prominent in motivating behaviour. These needs are for love, friendship and social interaction. We look for an environment where we are understood, respected and wanted. That is one reason for 'polarization' where people of similar background and beliefs tend to group together "love my neighbour" has perhaps a profound meaning.

4. *Esteem Needs*

This is an urge for achievement, prestige, status and power. It includes a desire for self-respect and the respect of others. Self-respect is the internal recognition. The respect from others is the external recognition and appreciation of one's contribution. This would affect self-confidence, independence, status, reputation, and prestige.

5. *Self-actualisation Needs*

This is the highest level of need in Maslows hierarchy and is the need for self-fulfilment to realize one's capacities and potentialities. The person seeks challenging work assignments that allows for creativity and opportunities for personal growth and advancement. This need is soul-searching and inner-oriented. A self-actualised person is creative, independent, content, spontaneous and has a good perception of reality, and the person is constantly striving to realize his full potential.

Maslow's Theory made management aware that people are motivated by a wide variety of needs and management must provide and opportunity to satisfy these needs through creating a physical and conceptual work environment so that people will be motivated to achieve organisational goals.

The management may cater to psychological needs by offering adequate wages and salary, acceptable working hours and working conditions; like heat ventilation, rest rooms, lighting, etc. Some bonuses and fringe benefits will be motivational.

The second level need of safety and security can be satisfied by management's initiative to provide life insurance, job security, medical insurance, cost of living increment, pension plans, etc.

The economic security, to some degree, in the form of minimum wages, unemployment benefits, welfare benefits, and safety is provided by law and other agencies. In addition the business and industrial environment provides basis for satisfying the first two needs. Hence management must create an atmosphere to satisfy higher level needs by taking the following steps:

(a) *To Satisfy Social Needs*

   (i) Provide opportunities for employees to interact, by providing coffee breaks, lunch facilities and recreational activities like picnic, etc.

   (ii) Create team spirit by keeping work groups informal wherever possible.

   (iii) Conduct periodic meetings with all subordinates.

(b) *To Satisfy Esteem Needs*

   (i) Design more challenging tasks and provide positive feedback on performance of employees.

   (ii) Give recognition and encouragement for performance and contribution and delegate additional authority to subordinates.

   (iii) Involve subordinates in goal setting and decision-making process.

   (iv) Provide adequate training and executive development to help the employee successfully accomplish his goals and increase the competency on the job.

   (v) Some of the symbol status that management can provide are job title, privileged parking, private secretary, promotion, company car, stock options, etc.

(c) *To Satisfy Self-Actualisation Needs*

   (i) The employees should be given an opportunity to shape their own jobs.

   (ii) Give the employees the freedom of expression.

   (iii) Encourage and develop creativity.

   (iv) Provide meaningful work that requires the development and use of full potential.

2. *Herzberg' Two Factor Theory of Motivation*

This is an environmental motivation theory which emphasises factors in the environment that contribute to the behaviour. His two factors are job satisfaction and job dissatisfaction. His conclusions are based on research conducted among 200 accountants and engineers.

Hygiene Factors

The hygiene factors do not motivate people. They simply maintain status quo. They produce no growth but they prevent loss. The absence of these factors leads to job satisfaction. The elimination of dissatisfaction does not mean satisfaction and they simply maintain a "Zero level of motivation". These factors are primarily extrinsic and environment-oriented and relate to job context, rather than job content. Some of the hygiene factors are:

- *(i)* Interpersonal relations with peers and supervisors and subordinates.
- *(ii)* Company policies and administration rules.
- *(iii)* Working conditions and job security.
- *(iv)* Supervisor's technical competence.
- *(v)* Salary and certain types of employee benefits.

All these factors are designed to avoid damage to efficiency or morale and these do not stimulate positive growth.

The word "hygiene" is taken from the medical field, where it means taking steps to maintain your health and not necessarily improve it. Similarly, hygiene factors in this theory of motivation prevent decay but does not encourage growth.

Hawthrone experiments suggests that improvements in working conditions or increments in financial benefits do not contribute to motivate performance. A new plant or new facilities at a plant seldom motivates workers if the workers do not enjoy their work and is no substitute for employee feelings or recognition and achievement.

Motivational Factors

These factors are related to the nature of work itself (job content), and are intrinsic to the job itself. These factors have a positive influence on morale, satisfaction, efficiency and higher productivity. Some of these factors are:

(a) *The Jobs Itself*

To be motivated, the people must like and enjoy their jobs. They are highly committed to goal achievement and do not mind to work after working hours to do what is to be done. Their moral is high as evidenced by lack of absenteeism and tardiness.

(b) *Recognition*

Recognition of an employee's contribution is highly morale boosting. It gives the workers a feeling of work and self-esteem. It is human nature to be happy when appreciated. This is the fourth level need in Maslow's model of hierarchical needs and boosts the ego and esteem factors.

(c) *Achievement*

A goal achievement gives a great feeling of accomplishment. The goal must be challenging requiring initiative and creativity. The opportunities must exist for a meaningful achievement, otherwise workers become sensitized to their environment and begin to find faults with it.

(d) *Responsibility*

It is an obligation to carry out the assigned duties satisfactorily. The higher the level of these duties, the more responsible you feel and more motivated you are. It is good feeling to know that you are considered a person of integrity and intelligence to be given a higher responsibility. It is a motivational factor that helps growth.

(e) *Growth and Advancement*

These factors are all inter-related and are positively related to motivation. Job promotions, higher responsibility, participation in central decision-making, executive benefits are all signs of growth and advancement and add to dedication and commitment of employees.

Herzberg's two factor model is tied in with Maslow's basic model in that the hygiene factors satisfy the first three levels of Maslow models of physiological needs, security and safety needs and social needs, and the motivational factors satisfy the last two higher level needs of esteem and self-actualization needs in the Maslow model.

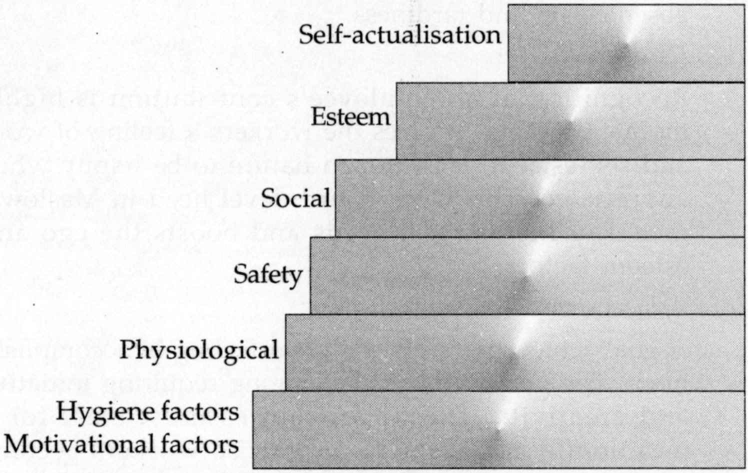

This theory has contributed to one management programme that has lent itself to the enhancement of motivators. This programme is that of "job enrichment" which means restructuring of jobs to include satisfier factors into the job content. Some of the principles of job enrichment are advanced by Herzberg himself:

(i) Give the employee the freedom of operation and responsibility. An opportunity to schedule one's own work enhances a sense of achievement and motivation. Expand his authority while retaining some controls and accountability for actions and results.

(ii) To increase responsibility, give the person a whole unit to operate. This unit may be one group, section or division and grant additional authority to achieve the group goal. This will help the growth and advancement factors.

(iii) Introduce new and more difficult tasks at each step giving the workers an opportunity to learn and specialize.

(iv) The employee must be given frequent feedback on his performance and on his handling of his own duties and responsibilities. This feedback will reinforce the learning process and reduce or eliminate any existing deviations and will appraise the employee about his progress.

3. *Vroom's Expectancy Model*

This model is based upon the assumption that the man is a rational being and will try to maximise his pay off. He will choose an alternative that would give him the most benefit. The theory is based on an individual's perception that a certain type of behaviour will lead to a certain type of outcome and his personal preference for that type of outcome. There are certain elements of this model:

(a) Expectancy

This is person's perceptions of the likelihood of a particular outcome resulting from a particular behaviour or action. The likelihood is probabilistic in nature and describes the relationship between an act and an outcome. For example, if a person works hard, he may expect a pay raise or just a promotion with a certain degree of likelihood for each of these two outcomes.

(b) Instrumentality

This factor relates to person's belief and expectations that his performance will lead to a particular desired regard. It is the degree of association of first level outcome of a particular effort to the second level outcome, which is the ultimate reward. For example, working hard may lead to better performance, which is first level outcome, which may result in reward, which is the second level outcome. If a person believes that his high performance will not be recognised or lead to expected rewards he will not be motivated to work hard for better output.

(c) *Valence*

This is the value a person assigns to his desired reward. He may not be willing to work hard to improve performance, if the reward for such improved performance is not what he desires. It is not the actual value of the reward but the perceptual value of the reward in the mind of the worker, that is important. A person may be motivated to work hard, not to get pay raise but to get recognition and status. Another person may be more interested in job security than status.

Accordingly, according to his model of motivation, the person's level of effort (motivation) depends upon:

Expectancy: A worker must be confident that his efforts will result in better productivity and that he has the ability to perform the task well.

Instrumentality: The worker must be confident that such high performance will be instrumental in getting desired rewards.

Valence: The worker must value these rewards as desired and satisfactory.

Hence the motivation is related to all these three factors as: Motivation force M = Expectancy E, × Instrumentality I, × Valence V.

As the relationship suggests the motivational force will be highest when expectancy, instrumentality and valence are all high. The management must recognise and determine the situation as it exists and take steps to improve upon these factors for behaviour modification. If a worker exhibits a poorly motivated behaviour it could be due to:

(i) *Low Effort-Performance Expectancy*

The worker may lack the necessary skills and training in order to believe that his extra efforts will lead to better performance. The management could provide opportunities for training to improve skills in order to improve the relationship between effort and performance.

(ii) *Low Performance-Reward Instrumentality Relationship*

Similar performance may not lead to similar rewards. The reward policy may be inconsistent and may depend upon factors other than simply the performance, which the worker may not be aware of or may not consider fair. The performance appraisal methods and the associated performance rewards may not be equitable. The management must re-evaluate the appraisal techniques and formulate policies that strengthens performance-reward relationship as just and equitable.

(iii) *Low Reward Valence*

Since the managers may look at the value of a reward differently than the worker, the management must investigate the desirability of the rewards which are given on the basis of performance. While monetary benefits may be more desirable for some workers, the need to be formally appreciated may be more valuable rewards for others for similar task-oriented achievements.

The Vroom's model tries to explain as to what factors affect a person's choice of a particular course of action among all available alternatives and why a person will be better motivated toward achievement of certain goals.

4. *Theory X or Y–Douglas McGregor*

Douglas McGregor stressed the importance of a manager clarifying his assumptions about the nature of man within the work situation. If a manager understood his subordinates, he would be able to select a motivational network that would better direct effort toward desired goals. He has given, names Theory 'X' and Theory 'Y' to time theories most often held about man and motivation.

A manager who fits into the Theory X group leans toward an organisational climate of close control, centralized authority, autocratic leadership, the minimum participation in the decision-making process. Such a manager makes certain assumptions which according to McGregor are:

1. Time average human being dislikes work and will avoid it to the extent he can.
2. Most people have to be forced or threatened by punishment to get them to make the effort necessary to accomplish organisational goals.
3. The average individual is basically passive and therefore prefers to directed rather than to assume any risk or responsibility. Above all he prefers security.

Theory Y manager operates with a different set of assumptions. He believes that effective organisational climate has greater decentralization of authority, less reliance on coercion and control, a democratic leadership style and more participation in time decision process. The assumption on which this type of organisational climate is based are:

1. The expenditure of physical and mental effort in work is as natural as play or rest. The average human being does not inherently dislike work. Depending upon controllable conditions, work may be a source of satisfaction (and will be voluntarily performed by source of punishment (and will be avoided if possible).
2. Extent of control and the threat of punishment are not the only means for bringing about effort towards organisational objectives. Man will exercise self-direction and self-control in the service of objectives to which he is committed.
3. Commitment of objectives is a function of the rewards associated with their achievement. The most significant of such reward, i.e. the satisfaction of ego and self-actualisation needs, can be direct products of effort directed toward organisational objectives.

4. The average human being tears under proper conditions, not only to accept but to seek responsibility. Avoidance of responsibility, lack of ambition, and emphasis on security are generally consequences of experience, not inherent human characteristics.
5. The capacity of exercise, a relatively high degree of imagination, ingenuity and creativity is the solution of organisational problems in widely, not narrowly disturbed the population.
6. Under the conditions of modern industrial life, the intellectual potentialities of the average human being are only partially utilised.

These assumptions involve sharply different implications for managerial strategy than do those of Theory X. Whereas Theory X offers management an easy rationalization for ineffective organisational performance. Theory Y holds management's methods of organisation and control responsible for lazy, indifferent, unwilling, uncreative, uncooperative employees, etc.

Motivators

Arch Patton, who did tremendous work on motivation has identified the following motivators:

1. *The Challenge We Find in Work*

   If this is to be maximised a man must know the purpose and scope of his responsibilities; what his authority is, what is expected of his and have a belief in the value of what he is doing.

2. *Status*

   Although recognised for centuries in church, military and government, industry, has come to recognise it only in recent years, it includes titles, promotions, and such symbols as office size and appointment 'executive' secretary, company car and club memberships.

3. *The Urge to Achieve Leadership*

   While difficult at times to distinguish from power it is really a desire to be a leader among one's fellow men.

4. *The Lash of Competition*

   This important motivating factor is present, in many aspects of life.

5. *Fear*

   This takes many forms, including fear of errors, of loss of a job or reduction of a bonus.

6. *Money*

   While placed last, this by means indicated that it is the least effective motivator; quite the contrary, it is most often more than more more money, being generally a reflection of other motivators.

The other motivators are security of job, search for identity, providing authority, and promotional opportunities.

Summary

- The organization goal can be achieved by motivation, the purpose of which is to create a congenial climate as well as physical work environment. The central idea of motivation is the will to work.
- There are contributions in the form of theories regarding motivation.

Self-Learning Activity

Try to answer the following questions on your own:

1. What do you mean by motivation?
2. Write about needs hierarchy theory.
3. Explain motivators.

5

Group Dynamics

Because the management of organizational behaviour is above all else a social endeavor, managers need a strong working knowledge of interpersonal behaviour. Research consistently reveals the importance of social skills for both individual and organizational success. "A derailed executive is one who, having reached the general manager level, finds that there is little chance of future advancement due to a misfit between job requirements and personal skills". The four reasons are as follows:

1. Problems with interpersonal relationships
2. Failure to meet business objectives
3. Failure to build and lead a team
4. Inability to change or adapt during a transition.

Let us begin by defining the term group in order to examine the types of groups, functions of group members, social exchanges in the workplace, and the group development process. Our attention then turns to group roles and norms, the basic building blocks of group dynamics. Effects of group structure and member characteristics on group outcomes are explored next. Finally, three serious threats to group effectiveness are discussed.

Groups and Social Exchanges

Groups and teams are inescapable features of modern life. College students are teamed with their peers for class projects. Parents serve on community advisory boards at their local high school. Managers find themselves on product planning committees and productivity task forces. Productive organizations simply cannot function without gathering individuals into groups and teams. Experience shows that group effort can bring out both the best and the worst in people. There are jokes on committees, e.g. a committee is a place where they take minutes and waste hours; a camel is a horse designed by a committee. Such jokes exist because committees all too often are plagued by lack of direction and by conflict. Modern managers need a solid understanding of groups and group processes so as to both avoid their pitfalls and tap their vast potential.

A group is defined as two or more freely interacting individuals who share collective norms and goals and have a common identity.

Formal and Informal Groups

Individuals join groups, or are assigned to groups, to accomplish various purposes. If the group is formed by a manager to help the organization accomplish its goals, then it qualifies as a formal group. Formal groups typically wear such labels as work group, team, committee, quality circle, or task force. An informal group exists when the members' overriding purpose of getting together is friendship or common interests. Although formal and informal groups often overlap some employees are not friends with their co-workers. The desirability of overlapping formal and informal groups is problematic. Some managers firmly believe that personal friendship fosters productive teamwork on the job while others view workplace "bull sessions" as a serious threat to productivity. Both situations are common, and it is the manager's job to strike a workable balance, based on the maturity and goals of the people involved.

Functions of Formal Groups

Researchers point out that formal groups fulfill two basic functions: organizational and individual. Complex combinations of these functions can be found in formal groups at any given time.

Social Exchanges in the Workplace

Social relationships are complex, alive, and dynamic. Accordingly, we need dynamic models for realistic understanding. A team of researchers from Auburn University recently proposed the instructive model and they call it the Workplace Social Exchange Network (WSEN) because it captures multilevel social exchanges within organizations, along with the complex network of variables affecting those exchanges.

(a) The exchange of currencies

The economic notion of exchange is at the heart of this model. In starkest economic terms, people exchange their time and labor for money when they take a job. But as this model realistically shows, there is much more at stake than just the exchange of time and labor for money. Individuals, organizations, and teams have many "currencies" they can grant or withhold.

The only social exchange of currency that is not self explanatory is "citizenship". Organizational citizenship involves going above and beyond what is expected (e.g., voluntarily working late to finish an important project), in short, being a good citizen.

(b) Three types of social exchange

According to the WSEN model, every employee has social exchanges on three levels: with the organization, with the boss, and with the work team as a whole. From the individual's perspective, exchanges at the various levels can be favorable or unfavorable. They can be motivating or demotivating, depending on the perceived equity of the exchange. For example, someone may have high-quality exchanges with his or her supervisor and work team, and be loyal to them. However, because the organization has a reputation for massive layoffs, the employee-organization exchange would be perceived unfavorably, thus fostering dissatisfaction and possibly poor performance and turnover.

(c) ***Situational factors***

The WSEN model includes three intervening factors: organizational structure, organizational culture, and employee needs. Structure, in the form of reporting relationships, policies, and work rules, shapes the individual's expectations about what is fair and what is unfair. So, too, cultural norms and traditions create a context for judging the fairness of social exchanges. The individual's need profile will determine which of the organization's exchange currencies are motivating and which are not. People are motivated when they have a realistic chance of having their needs satisfied.

Is the social exchange relevant? Finally, at the bottom center of the WSEN model is the individual's perceptual filter. Is the particular social exchange salient or relevant? Salient stimuli tend to capture and dominate one's attention. An exchange between the employee and his or her organization, leader, or team needs to be salient if it is to influence the behaviour. For example if a marketing assistant is indifferent to her teammates on a special project, that particular exchange would not be salient or relevant for her. Overall, the WSEN model does a good job of building a conceptual bridge between motivation theories and group dynamics. Also, it realistically indicates the multilevel nature of social relationships within organizations.

Group Development Process

Groups and teams in the workplace go through a maturation process, such as one would find in any life-cycle situation (e.g., humans, organizations, products). While there is general agreement among theorists that the group development process occurs in identifiable stages, they disagree about the exact number, sequence, length, and nature of those stages. One oft-cited model is the one proposed in 1965 by educational psychologist Bruce W. Tuckman. His original model involved only four stages (forming, storming, norming and performing). The five stage model evolved when Tuckman and a doctoral student added "adjourning" in 1977.

Tuckman's theory has been repeated and taught so often and for so long that many have come to view it as documented fact, not merely a theory.

The five stages Tuckman's model notice, how individuals give up a measure of their independence when they join and participate in a group. The various stages are not necessarily of the same duration or intensity. For instance, the storming stage may be practically nonexistent or painfully long, depending on the goal clarity and the commitment and maturity of the members.

Stage 1: Forming

During this ice-breaking stage, group members tend to be uncertain and anxious about such things as their roles, who is in charge, and the group's goals. Mutual trust is low, and there is a good deal of holding back to see who takes charge and how. If the formal leader (e.g. a supervisor) does not assert his or her authority, an emergent leader will eventually step in to fulfill the group's need for leadership and direction. Leaders typically mistake this honeymoon period (the emergent leader's) as a mandate for permanent control. But later problems may force a leadership change.

Stage 2: Storming

This is time of testing. Individuals test the leader's policies and assumptions as they try to determine how they fit into the power structure. Subgroups take shape, and subtle forms of rebellion, such as procrastination, occur. Many groups stall in Stage 2 because power polices erupts into open rebellion.

Stage 3: Norming

Groups that make it through Stage 2 generally do so because a respected member, other than the leader, challenges the group to resolve its power struggles so something can be accomplished. Questions about authority and power are resolved through unemotional, matter-of-fact group discussion. A feeling of team spirit is experienced because members believe they have found their proper roles. *Group cohesiveness*, defined as the "we feeling" that binds members of a group together, is the principal by-product of stage 3.

Stage 4: Performing

Activity during this vital stage is focused on solving task problems. As members of a mature group, contributors get their work done without hampering others. There is a climate of open communication, strong cooperation, and lots of helping behaviour. Conflicts and job boundary disputes are handled constructively and efficiently. Cohesiveness and personal commitment to group goals help the group to achieve more than could any one individual acting alone.

Stage 5: Adjourning

The work is done; it is time to move on to other things. Having worked so hard to get along and get something done, many members feel a compelling sense of loss. The return to independence can be eased by rituals celebrating "the end" and "new beginning". Leaders need to emphasize valuable lessons learned in group dynamics to prepare everyone for future group and team efforts.

Roles and Norms

Social building blocks for group and organizational behaviour

Work groups transform individuals into functioning organizational members through subtle yet powerful social forces. These social forces, in effect, turn "I" into "we" and "me" into "us". Group influence weaves individuals into the organization's social fabric by communicating and enforcing both role expectations and norms. We need to understand roles and norms if we are to effectively manage group and organizational behaviour.

ROLES

"Roles are sets of behaviours that persons expect of occupants of a position. Role theory attempts to explain how these social expectations influence employee behaviour. This section explores role theory by analyzing a role episode and defining the terms role overload, role conflict, and role ambiguity.

Role episodes

In any given role episode (Fig. 5.1), there is a role sender and a focal person who is expected to act out the role. Within a broader context, one may be simultaneously a role sender and a focal person. For the sake of social analysis, however, it is instructive to deal with separate role episodes.

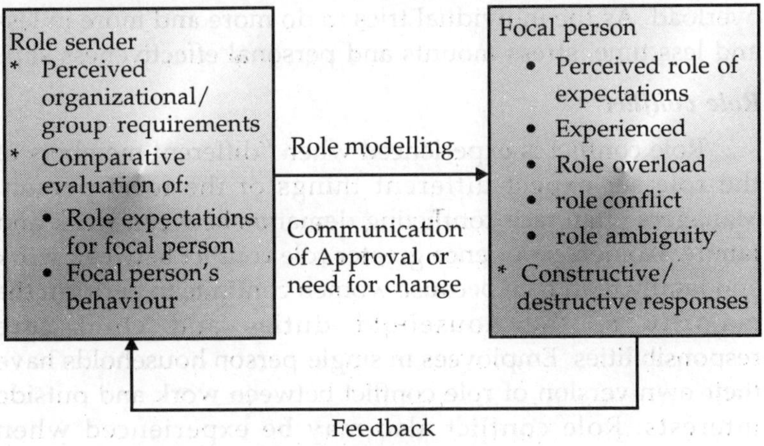

***Fig. 5.1:* A Role Episode**

Role episodes begin with the role sender's perception of the relevant organization's or group's behavioural requirements. Those requirements serve as a standard for formulating expectations for the focal person's behaviour. The role sender then cognitively evaluates the focal person's actual behaviour against those expectations. Appropriate verbal and behavioural messages are then sent to the focal person to pressure him or her into behaving as expected.

On the receiving end of the role episode, the focal person accurately or inaccurately perceives the communicated role expectations and modeled behaviour. Various combinations of role overload, role conflict, and role ambiguity are then experienced. The focal person then responds constructively by engaging in problem solving, for example, or destructively because of undue tension, stress, and strain.

Role overload

Role overload occurs when "the sum total of what role senders expect of the focal person far exceeds what he or she is able to do. Students who attempt to handle a full course load and maintain a decent social life while working 30 or more hours a week know fully well the consequences of role overload. As the individual tries to do more and more in less and less time, stress mounts and personal effectiveness slip.

Role conflict

Role conflict is experienced when "different members of the role set expect different things of the focal person. Managers often face conflicting demands between work and family. Women experience greater role conflict between work and family than men because women continue to perform the majority of the household duties and child care responsibilities. Employees in single-person households have their own version of role conflict between work and outside interests. Role conflict also may be experienced when internalized values, ethics, or personal standards collide with others' expectations.

Role ambiguity

Those who experience role conflict may have trouble complying with role demands, but they at least know what is expected of them. Role ambiguity occurs when "members of the role set fail to communicate to the focal person expectations they have or information needed to perform the role, either because they do not have the information or because they deliberately withhold it. In short, people experience role ambiguity when they do not know what is expected of them. Organizational newcomers often complain about unclear job descriptions and vague promotion criteria. According to role theory, prolonged role ambiguity can foster job dissatisfaction, erode self-confidence, and hamper job performance.

Role ambiguity varies across cultures. People in individualistic cultures were found to have higher role ambiguity than people in collectivist cultures. Role outcomes typically are experienced in some combination, usually to the detriment of the individual and the organization. A study in Israel reveals lower job performance when employees experienced a combination of role conflict and role ambiguity.

NORMS

Norms are more encompassing than roles. While roles involve behavioural expectations for specific positions, norms help organizational members determine right from wrong and good from bad. "A norm is an attitude, opinion, feeling, or action-shared by two or more people - that guides their behaviour. Although norms are typically unwritten and seldom discussed openly, they have a powerful influence on group and organizational behaviour.

How norms are developed?

Experts say norms evolve in an informal manner as the group or organization determines what it takes to be effective. Norms develop in various combinations of the following four ways:

1. *Explicit statements by supervisors or co-workers*: For instance, a group leader might explicitly set norms about not drinking (alcohol) at lunch.
2. *Critical events in the group's history*: At times there is a critical event in the group's history that establishes as important precedent. (For example, a key recruit may have decided to work elsewhere because a group member said too many negative things about the organization. Hence, a norm against such "sour grapes" behaviour might evolve.)

3. *Primacy*: The first behaviour pattern that emerges in a group often sets group expectations. If the first group meeting is marked by very formal interaction between supervisors and employees, then the group often expects future meetings to be conducted in the same way.
4. *Carryover behaviours from past situations*: Such carryover of individual behaviours from past situations can increase the predictability of group members' behaviours in new settings and facilitate task accomplishment. For instance, students and professors carry fairly constant sets of expectations from class to class.

Why Norms are enforced

Norms tend to be enforced by group members when they:

- Help the group or organization survive.
- Clarify or simplify behavioural expectations.
- Help individuals avoid embarrassing situations.
- Clarify the group's or organization's central values and/ or unique identity.

Functional Roles Performed by Group Members

Task versus Maintenance Roles

Task roles: Task roles enable the work group to define, clarify, and pursue a common purpose, meanwhile, maintenance roles foster supportive and constructive interpersonal relationships. In short, task roles keep the group on track while maintenance roles keep the group together. A project team member is performing a task function when he or she stands at an update meeting and says, "What is the real issue here?" we don't seem to be getting anywhere, another individual who says, "let's hear from those who oppose this plan," is performing a maintenance function. Importantly, each of the various task and maintenance roles may be played in varying combinations and sequences by either the group's leader or any of its members.

Checklist for managers: The task and maintenance roles listed in Table 5.1 can serve as a handy checklist for managers and group leaders who wish to ensure proper group development. Roles that are not always performed when needed, such as those of coordinator, evaluator, and gatekeeper, can be performed in a timely manner by the formal leader or assigned to other members. The task roles of initiator, orienter, and energizer are especially important because they are goal-directed roles.

Table 5.1: Functional Roles Performed by Group Members

Task Roles	Description
Initiator	Suggests new goals or ideas.
Information seeder/giver	Clarifies key issues.
Opinion seeker/giver	Clarifies pertinent values.
Elaborator	Promotes greater understanding through examples or exploration of implication.
Coordinator	Pulls together ideas and suggestions.
Orienter	Keeps group headed toward its stated goal(s).
Evaluator	Tests group's accomplishments with various criteria such as logic and practicality.
Energizer	Prods group to move along or to accomplish more.
Procedural technician	Performs routine duties (e.g. handing out materials or rearranging seats).
Recorder	Performs a "function by documenting discussion and outcomes".
Maintenance Roles	**Description**
Encourager	Fosters group solidarity by accepting and praising various points of view.
Harmonizer	Mediates conflict through reconciliation or humor.
Compromiser	Helps resolve conflict by meeting others half way.
Gatekeeper	Encourages all group members to participate.
Standard setter	Evaluates the quality of group processes.
Commentator	Records and comments on group processes dynamics.
Follower	Serves as a passive audience.

Threats to Group Effectiveness

Even when managers carefully staff and organize task groups, group dynamics can still go haywire. The three major threats to group effectiveness include:

1. The Asch effect;
2. Groupthink; and
3. Social loafing.

It can help managers take necessary preventive steps. The first two problems relate to blind conformity.

Very little would be accomplished in task groups and organizations without conformity to norms, role expectations, policies, and rules and regulations. After all, deadlines, commitments, and product/service quality standards have to be established and adhered to if the organization is to survive.

Excessive or blind conformity can stifle critical thinking, the last line of defense against unethical conduct. Managers need to understand the mechanics of blind conformity.

The Asch Effect

Fifty-one years ago, social psychologist Solomon Asch conducted a series of laboratory experiments that revealed a negative side of group dynamics. Under the guise of a "Perception test", Asch had groups of seven to nine volunteer college students look at 12 pairs of cards such as the ones. The object was to identify the line that was the same length as the standard line. Each individual was told to announce his or her choice to the group. Since the differences among the comparison lines were obvious, there should have been unanimous agreement during each of the 12 rounds. But that was not the case.

A minority of one: All but one member of each group were Asch's confederates who agreed to systematically select the wrong line during seven of the rounds (the other five rounds were control rounds for comparison purposes). The remaining individual was the native subject who was being tricked. Group pressure was created by having the naïve subject in each group be among the last to announce his or her choice. Thirty-one subjects were tested. Asch's research question was; "How often would the naïve subjects conform to a majority opinion that was obviously wrong?

Only 20 per cent of Asch's subjects remained entirely independent; 80 per cent yielded to the pressures of group opinion at least once! Fifty-eight per cent knuckled under to the "immoral majority" at least twice. Hence, the Asch effect, the distortion of individual judgment by a unanimous but incorrect opposition, was documented. (Do you ever turn your back on your better judgment by giving in to group pressure?)

A managerial perspective: The Asch effect can be observed in any culture. Both high and low degrees of blind conformity have been observed with various situations and subjects. Internationally, collectivist countries, where the group prevails over the individual, produced higher levels of conformity than individualistic countries. The point is not precisely how great the Asch effect is in a given situation or culture, but rather, managers committed to ethical conduct need to be concerned that the Asch effect exists.

Even isolated instances of blind, unthinking conformity seriously threaten the effectiveness and integrity of work groups and organizations. Ethical codes mentioning specific practices also can provide support and guidance.

Groupthink

Janis defines groupthink as "a mode of thinking that people engage in when they are deeply involved in a cohesive in-group when members' strivings for unanimity override their motivation to realistically appraise alternative courses of action". He adds, "Groupthink refers to deterioration of mental efficiency, reality testing, and moral judgment that results from in-group pressures". Unlike Asch's, subjects, who were strangers to each other, members of groups victimized by groupthink are friendly, tightly knit, and cohesive.

Symptoms of Groupthink

1. *Invulnerability:* An Illusion that breeds excessive optimism and risk taking.
2. *Inherent morality:* A belief that encourages the group to ignore ethical implications.
3. *Rationalization:* Protects per assumptions.
4. *Stereotyped views of opposition:* Cause group to underestimate opponents.
5. *Self-censorship:* Stifles critical debate.
6. *Illusion of unanimity:* Silence interpreted to mean consent.
7. *Peer pressure:* Loyalty of dissenters is questioned.
8. *Mind guards:* Self-appointed protectors against adverse information.

→

Decision-making defects

1. Few alternatives.
2. No re-examination of preferred alternatives.
3. No re-examination of rejected alternatives.
4. Rejection of expert opinions.
5. Selective bias of new information.
6. No contingency plans.

Fig. 5.2: **Symptoms of Groupthink Lead to Defective Decision Making**

In short, policy- and decision-making groups can become so cohesive that strong-willed executives are able to gain unanimous support for poor decisions.

Groupthink prevention studies reveal that:

- ❖ Groups with a moderate amount of cohesiveness produce better decisions than low or high-cohesive groups.
- ❖ Highly cohesive groups victimized by groupthink make the poorest decisions, despite high confidence in those decisions.

Janis believes prevention is better than cure when dealing with groupthink. He recommends the following preventive measures:

1. Each member of the group should be assigned the role of critical evaluator. This role involves activity voicing objections and doubts.
2. Top-level executives should use policy committees to rubber-stamp decisions that have already been made.
3. Different groups with different leaders should explore the same policy questions.
4. Sub-group debates and outside experts should be used to introduce fresh perspectives.
5. Someone should be given the role of devil's advocate when discussing major alternatives. This person tries to uncover every conceivable negative factor.
6. Once a consensus has been reached, everyone should be encouraged to rethink their position to check for flaws.

Social Loafing

Is group performance less than, equal to or greater than the sum of its parts? Can three people, for example, working together accomplish less than, the same as, or more than they would working separately? An interesting study conducted more than a half century ago by a French agricultural engineer named Ringelmann found the answer to be "less than". In a rope-pulling exercise, Ringelmann reportedly found that three people pulling together could achieve only two and a half times the average individual rate. Eight pullers achieved less than four times the individual rate. This tendency for individual effort to decline as group size increases has come to be called *social loafing*.

Let us briefly analyze this threat to group effectiveness and synergy with an eye toward avoiding it.

Social Loafing Theory and Research

Among the theoretical explanations for the social loafing effect are:

1. Equity of effort ("Everyone else is goofing off, so why shouldn't I?")

2. Loss of personal accountability ("I'm lost in the crowd, so who cares?")
3. Motivational loss due to the sharing of rewards ("Why should I work harder than the others when everyone gets the same reward?")
4. Coordination loss as more people perform the task ("We're getting in each other's way").

Laboratory studies refined these theories by identifying situational factors that moderated the social loafing effect. Social loafing occurred when:

❖ The task was perceived to be unimportant, simple, or not interesting.

❖ Group members thought their individual output was not identifiable.

❖ Group members expected their co-workers to loaf.

But social loafing did not occur when group members in two laboratory studies expected to be evaluated. Also, research suggests that self-reliant "individualists" are more prone to social loafing than group-oriented "collectivists". But individualists can be made more cooperative by keeping the group small and holding each member personally accountable for results.

Practical Implications:

These findings demonstrate that social loafing is not an inevitable part of group effort. Management can curb this threat to group effectiveness by making sure the task is challenging and perceived as important. Additionally, it is a good idea to hold group members personally accountable for identifiable portions of the group's task.

Group	:	Two or more freely interacting people with shared norms and goals and a common identity
Formal group	:	Formed by the organization.
Informal group	:	Formed by friends or those with common interests.

Group cohesiveness	:	A "we feeling" binding group members together.
Role overload	:	Others' expectations exceed one's ability.
Role conflict	:	Others have conflicting or inconsistent expectations.
Norm	:	Shared attitudes, opinions, feelings, or actions that guide social behaviour.
Task roles	:	Task-oriented group behaviour.
Maintenance roles	:	Relationship-building group behaviour.
Asch effect	:	Giving in to a unanimous but wrong opposition.
Groupthink	:	Janis's term for a cohesive in-group's unwillingness to realistically view alternatives.

Summary

- A group is defined as two or more freely interacting individuals who share collective norms and goals and have a common identity.
- It is a good idea to hold group members personally accountable for identifiable portions of the group's task.

Self-Learning Activity

Try to answer the following questions on your own:

1. Discuss about group development process.
2. Explain role ambiguity.
3. Describe Asch Effect.

6

Communication

Definition

William Scott defines:

"It is a process which involves the transmission and accurate replication of ideas ensured by feedback for the purpose of eliciting actions which will accomplish organisational goals".

Communication is a vital part of direction function. Through communication messages are sent and received. To communicate is to inform to show or to spread information. It is the means by which management gets its job done. Lawrence Apply points out the communication process as follows:

1. Clarifying the idea or problem.
2. Getting participation in developing a solution to the problem.
3. Transmitting ideas or decisions.
4. Motivating others to take action agreed upon.
5. Measuring the effectiveness of communication.

Elements in the Process of Communication

The process of communication comprises three elements:

1. The communicator or sender;

2. The message; and
3. The receiver.

1. *The Communicator or Sender*

In an organisational set-up, the communicator or sender is the employee with ideas, intentions, opinions, information and a purpose for communicating.

2. *The Message*

The purpose of the communicator or sender is expressed in the form of a message—either verbal or non-verbal.

3. *The Receiver*

In order that the process of communication is completed, the message in its relevant form is transmitted to the receiver.

Importance of Communication

1. Every aspect of manager's job, may it be planning, organizing, staffing, directing and controlling involves communication. Most of the time of the managers is spent in communicating. No wonder, according to expert's research finding, a manager spends 75 to 90 per cent of his time in communicating, exchanging information with people.
2. Nothing contributes so much to managerial effectiveness as effective communication.
3. However, the decisions at the top are, they will serve no purpose unless the manager can successfully communicate the implications of these decisions to the subordinates who are to implement them.
4. Communication, is the essence of organised activity. It is the basis of direction and leadership. The managers have to communicate to give instructions, orders to assign jobs and fix responsibilities.
5. Communication renders the complexity of business intelligible and workable.
6. The better the communication, the more efficient the work performance.

Objectives of Communication

1. To develop information and understanding among all workers.
2. To foster an attitude which is necessary for motivation, cooperation and job satisfaction.
3. To discourage misinformation, ambiguity and rumors.
4. To prepare workers for a change in methods or environment by giving them the necessary information in advance.
5. To encourage subordinates to supply ideas and suggestions for improving upon the product or work environment, and taking these suggestions seriously.
6. To improve labour-management relations by keeping the communication channels open.
7. To encourage social relations among workers by encouraging inter-communication.

Methods of Communication in Management

Guidelines suggested by Keith Davis may do much to improve written communications:

- Use simple words and phrases.
- Use short and familiar words.
- Use personal pronouns (such as 'you') whenever appropriate.
- Give illustrations and examples; use charts.
- Use short sentences and paragraphs.
- Use active verbs such as 'The manager plans'
- Economize on adjectives.
- Express thoughts logically and in a direct way.
- Avoid unnecessary words.

Communication Process

A simple communication process model can be described as consisting of the following steps:

Message Sender

This is the source of information or the imitator of the communication.

Encoding

In this step the ideas to be conveyed are encoded into series of symbols or gestures, or some other format of expression.

The Message

The message is a physical form of the thought which can be experienced and understood by one or more senses of the receiver. It would be in the form of hearing, or other physical gestures.

Channel of Communication

It is a vehicle used for the transmission of the message. The channel bridges the gap between the sender and the receiver. It may be a face to face conversation, telephone conversation, a written form or through any form of gestures.

Perception of the Message

The message is received by the person for whom it was meant and he becomes the receiver of the message.

Decoding Process

The receiver decodes the message for the purpose of interpreting and understanding the meaning of the message, the more effective the communication.

Action

This is a response from the receiver who has received and accepted the communication. This may be compliance with an instruction, or simply filling of the message for future references.

Principles of Good Communication–7C's

The American Professors Frank Groves and Richard Vilstrup give the seven C's of communication.

1. *Credibility*

Communication starts with a climate of belief. This is built by performance on the part of the source. The receiver must have confidence in the sender. He must have a high regard for the source's competence on the subject.

2. *Context*

A communication programme must square with the realities of its environment. The context must provide for participation and play back. The context must confirm not contradict the message.

3. *Content*

The message must have meaning for the receiver and it must be compatible with his value system. It must have relevance to him. In general, people select those items of information which promise them generates rewards.

4. *Clarity*

The message must be put in simple terms. Words must mean the same thing to the receiver as they do to the sender. The farther a message has to travel, the simple it must be. An institution must speak with one voice, not many voices.

5. *Continuity and Consistency*

Communication is an unending process. It requires repetition to achieve penetration. The story must be consistent.

6. *Channels*

Established channels of communication should be used, channels which the receiver uses and respects. Creating new ones is difficult. Different channels have different effects and serve in different stages of the diffusion process.

7. *Capability of Audience*

Communication must take into account the capability of the audience. Communications are most effective when they require the least effort on the part of the recipient.

Barriers to Communication

Communication, which is sent must reach the receiver in time and it must be received in the form and in the same seriousness in which the sender is interested. Wrong communications or barriers to communications may tend to create misunderstanding, friction and even misinterpretation. Ultimately it may cause great damage to the enterprise. Koontz and O'Donnel give the following barriers to communication:

Badly Expressed Messages

The communication can be expressed using proper words and phrases. Lack of clarity and precision may lead to errors in communication.

Faulty Translations

If a communication is to be passed on to various people it must be translated to suit them.'It is often not enough to pass on a communication word for word; either it must be put into words appropriate to the framework in which the receiver operates, or it must be accomplished by an interpretation which will be understood by the receiver.

Loss by Transmission and Poor Retention

When communications are passed on from one stage to the other, the accuracy is lost. Oral communication has this danger. Equally important is retention of the message. It must be properly grasped.

Inattention

If an oral communication is sent and the listener is not attentive, it may lead to the failure.

Unclarified Assumptions

If the subordinate interprets a communication assuming differently, it may affect the process.

Insufficient Adjustment Period

When people work under different time, place, shifts, they may not have the time to receive the full meaning of the communication.

Distrust of Communication

Some times messages are changed over the original communication. Such change may delay action.

Premature Evaluation

Some executives may prematurely evaluate the communication, rather than "keep an uncompromised position during the interchange".

Fear

If the subordinates are not reporting the truth due to fear the communication gap may lead to severe consequences.

Failure to Communicate

Some times managers may not communicate due to sheer laziness or even to embarrass people deliberately.

Summary

- Communication is a vital part of direction function. Through communication messages are sent and received. To communicate is to inform to show or to spread information. It is the means by which management gets its job done.

Self-Learning Activity

Try to answer the following questions on your own:

1. What is the importance of communication?
2. Discuss the communication process.
3. What are the principles of good communication?

7

Perception and Attitudes

Perception is the process whereby people become aware of others and the world around them. In the course of their daily lives individuals form perceptions of people and events which they encounter. The individual receives information from various sources and then, by synthesizing and re-ordering that information, attempts to place some form of construct on it. This mental process thus helps to structure and develop an individual's awareness of his immediate environment. It represents the sum of the information received and the process of placing it in some kind of order.

PERCEPTION PROCESSES

Perception develops because the individual needs to relate to his environment and create some kind of perspective for himself. By this means he creates order out of chaos and produces a framework of reference which enables him to manage the multifarious sources of information received in a meaningful way. How an individual looks at his environment is, possibly, due as much to his social experience as it is to his psychological disposition. In practice, it may be difficult to ascertain the exact nature of the influences which underly the particular construct. The nature of perception is peculiar to each individual but basically perception is a process of interpreting reality, a process which in turn assists in the formation off attitudes and the development of patterns of consistent behaviour. Each person may have a unique view of what constitutes reality, and it is perception which enables an individual to use his past experience and understanding in the analysis and interpretation of a situation which ultimately enables coherence and organization to emerge for that person. One problem is that the view for one individual cannot be employed as though it represents reality for everyone else. Lack of appreciation of this factor is likely to lead to misunderstandings as to why contra views exist and, as a result, opportunity for realistic analysis of differences may be lost. Whatever factors are under consideration, we may simply not have sufficient information about them, and, therefore, by contributing our own interpretation, we attempt to perceive the situation. Inevitably, where a number of individuals are involved, different views will emerge. A further point to note is that individuals form and reform their own interpretations of a given situation until they achieve what is considered, by them, to be a satisfactory construction of the factors under consideration when an individual indicates a lack of understanding of another person's point of view. It may be that the individual is applying his own perceptions and points of reference and explanation of that other person's behaviour. This can make effective communication difficult, and processes of understanding, consultation and negotiation may be inhibited. Frequently, emotions may be involved and serve as a means of reinforcement to the process of developing perceptions. A sense of security is involved in the achievement of a satisfactory framework of reference and, therefore, the individual may be reluctant to abandon particular attitudes and behaviour which enhance his security. To this extent the individual may be selective in relation to his use of information facts and circumstances. He may tend towards selecting those factors which support his existing perceptions. By this means he retains his sense of security and is likely to reject or distort information which is incompatible with his views. This process may be viewed as acting at the level of the subconscious and should not necessarily be construed as pertaining to deliberate distortion. The individual seeks information which fits in with what his picture of reality already suggests is appropriate.

A further problem which may arise concerns the existence of distortion. The individual is faced by numerous events and circumstances, many of which cannot be ignored altogether. We have described the process of selectivity as affording one way in which the individual copes with his milieu. However, this particular process is only one of many and cannot inadequately describe all circumstances. Not all information reaching the individual can be rejected, and in this circumstance a new way of coping with the threat to security may emerge a process which involves distortion. Here, information is reorganized in such a way that it will fit the perceptual framework of the individual. The information has meaning only when related to the individual's particular view of the circumstances under consideration. Any item of information received which does not fit the pattern required may be reinterpreted in such a way as to make it fit. This process of modification, involving distortion, occurs subconsciously for much of the time and, as with selectivity, enables the individual to retain his feelings of order and security.

These examples illustrate some of the problems surrounding the communication process. Furthermore, if one individual is attempting to communicate a particular message to another, then the success of his communique may well depend on his understanding of how the message is likely to relate to the views and attitudes of the person with whom he is communicating. He has to try to put himself in the other person's shoes to attempt to achieve a construct of the information similar to the one being undertaken by that person. In practice this is a very difficult thing to achieve. It makes great demands on the individual in terms of his sensitivity to the needs of the other person and, in consciously striving to understand a viewpoint other than his own, he may have to abandon his own strongly held and cherished ideals. However, if the attempt is not made, then adequate communication becomes much harder to achieve, and this may have some influence on creating and sustaining effective relationships.

THEORIES OF PERCEPTION

The question arises as to how the process of perception works. One approach is to view it as being intuitive. For example, is the judgment immediate, following assimilation of facts and circumstances?

Theories concerned with intuition involve consideration of whether perception occurs directly, whether it is innate and whether it is total that is the individual identified or understood in terms of his whole personality.

One popular theory within the intuitive school is Gestalt theory. Fundamentally, this view propounds the notion that the whole is greater than the sum of its individual parts, and that the brain organizes or adds information to the other information inputs it receives. It relates to perception in that, for example, one individual in communication with another conveys to that person some knowledge of his psychic disposition. The information is conveyed through some physical expression such as a facial movement. The other person in the relationship sees this, and through his own psychic process can perceive and understand that individual. This is known as isomorphism.

Another view relates to the development of empathy between individuals in communication with each other. This theory states that one person understands how the other feels because he is able to visualize himself in a similar situation.

A second school of theory in relation to perception is concerned with the process of inference. This view considers that the individual creates his framework of references by a process of inference accrued from the knowledge available. For example, a proposition based on inference would work as follows:

1. Individuals with firm handshakes have strong characters.
2. This individual has a firm handshake.
3. This same individual is of strong character.

What has happened is that statement 3 is inferred from our perceptions surrounding statements 1 and 2. Our reasoning process has concluded that statement 3 is correct despite the absence of a complete direct link between it and the first two statements. Our perception has assumed that statement 3 is a reasonable one to adopt and derives its truth from our scan and interpretation of statement 1 and 2.

ATTITUDE FORMATION

We have discussed notions surrounding the concept of perception. To a considerable extent the latter is essential to the process of attitude formation. Attitude refers to a mental state whereby an individual is disposed towards a particular response in relation to people, objects and situations. This goes beyond how we might, for example, define personality. Attitudes are concerned with what an individual may like or dislike. It is likely that emotions will be involved and the actual emotive state of the individual at a given point of time may influence the formation of a particular attitude. The latter may be of short or long term duration, depending to some extent on whether emotion is the sole determinant or one of many such determinants which continue to exert considerable influence even when emotion itself is no longer involved. The development of attitudes is fundamental to many aspects of behaviour. Changes in behaviour are likely to be longer lasting where a change in attitude occurs, although the former can be achieved without the latter, perhaps by the use of some form of reward/punishment system. Attitude formation arises from many different sources. Some are cultural, others may be economic or social they may be derived from the group or groups in which the individual circulates and may form a consistent pattern with a high degree of consonance among them. The family, religious belief and education may all be influences which contribute to the state of consonance. A further consideration is that the logic which an individual adopts is relevant to himself, but not necessarily to others. Other people may view aspects of the behaviour of a person as demonstrating inconsistencies while the individual himself may simply not see them in this light. What represents rationality to one person may be seen as irrational by others. This suggests that knowledge in itself may be insufficient as a basis for attitude formation. It is the way in which the knowledge is used the rationalization process in to defend a particular view which is also an important factor in attitude development.

The history of research into attitudes, particularly attitude change, is a long and detailed one. In the field of social psychology, attitude research has been viewed as being of prime importance. In particular, Allport (1935) drew attention to its importance in enabling the development of social psychology as a definitive area of study. In a volume of this size it is impossible to adequately examine the total nature of theoretical studies in attitude change. However, when discussing perception, mention was made of the nature of Gestalt psychology with its essentially cognitive approach. In more recent times considerable attention has been given to the development of balance theories. Fundamentally, these are based on the premise that the individual attempts to achieve consistency among his various attitudes and that psychological pressures exist to arrange new information received in such a way that it fits with his existing attitudes. In particular, Festinger (1957) postulated a theory of cognitive dissonance. He examined various cognitive inputs received by the individual, recognizing that certain of these may be consonant to each other, that is, they are in agreement or have some basis of commonality, while others may be dissonant, i.e. out of agreement. It is the latter state which creates problems because, associated with this condition, is a degree of psychological unhappiness. For example, an individual may perceive trade unions as being undesirable and form unfavourable attitudes towards them. However, he may work within an environment where unionism is strongly supported. His cognitions in respect of this situation are dissonant, i.e. they are at odds with each other and are out of balance, and he will experience pressures to restore them to a state of balance. People desire cognitions which are consonant and therefore seek to find ways of achieving or re-achieving this state. In the example quoted, possibilities open to the individual include a situation where the individual disassociates himself from his work colleagues to such an extent that their views are no longer of significance. Here the discordant aspect is being removed or the individual changes his mind about unions so that they are then similar to those of his colleagues. His perceptions are then in a state of balance and psychological happiness is restored.

Much will depend on the degree of importance which the individual attaches to the particular issues and the extent to which he experiences unhappiness. The centrality of the attitude that is its importance to the individual, will have a considerable influence on whether that individual is willing to change his viewpoint and behaviour. If the level of importance is high, then dissonance may be tolerated despite the problems it brings.

Associated with the notion of attitude change is a concept which attempts to provide further explanation of the process. This is known as 'reinforcement theory' and is based on the proposition that if an individual behaves in a certain way, and such behaviour is rewarded, then he is more likely to behave in a similar way in the future. The usefulness of this consideration will depend to a large extent on the value that the particular individual places on the potential reward. However, it does present the possibility that an organization, through its management, can use the rewards at its disposal to influence the behaviour of subordinates. Of course, in practice, organizations do use rewards to commend behaviour which is regarded as appropriate. However, the nature of the influence involves a process of shaping the individual's responses in such a way that he will learn to co-operate, and carries with it anticipation that over a period of time such conditioning will result in the development of attitudes favourable to the organization's objectives.

ATTITUDES AND COMMUNICATION

The whole question of perception and attitude formation has considerable implication for communication as a control process within the organization. In terms of two people communicating with each other in a manager and subordinate relationship, each person in the transaction has something to gain from a situation where communication is effective. For the manager it enables the possibility of increasing the subordinate's understanding of the organization's objectives. For the subordinate, effective communication certain provides an opportunity to create a picture for himself of how he contributes to the organization's objectives, and how his role fits into the broader perspective of the total organization. Both parties can gain from improved understanding which itself must be influenced to a considerable degree by the processes of attitude formation, including the extent to which the constitution of reality is shared. However, it requires more than each party hearing what the other has to say. There has to be some degree of understanding which relates to the other person and some acceptance of what that understanding implies. This may involve a proposed course of action being modified to take account of what the other person requires.

Summary

- Perception and attitudes are closely related to motivation which is the subject of the next chapter. To consider motivation in isolation, devoid of considerations of perception and attitudes, would be to neglect provision of an adequate base for consideration of the topic.

Self-Learning Activity

Try to answer the following questions on your own:

1. What is perception?
2. Describe attitude formation.

8

Organization Goals

Organizations are defined in terms of two or more people uniting together to co-ordinate their activities in pursuit of a set of common goals. The pursuit of goals is fundamental to our definition of an organization and therefore requires some further examination. Etzioni (1964) defines an organization goal as 'a desired state of affairs which the organization attempts to realize'.

Why Organizations Have Goals

A goal or set of goals provide the foundation on which an organization is built. Goals serve a number of purposes:

1. Goals provide a yardstick against which to assess the performance of the organization. Two key performance measurements are often identified effectiveness and efficiency. Effectiveness is a measure of the success of the organization in attaining its goals, while efficiency is a measure of how well the organization has utilized its resources in attaining those goals. Efficiency is normally measured in terms of costs or productivity. While organizations which are effective are usually efficient, and vice versa, this may not always be the case. For example, a business organization whose goal is to maximize profits may be ineffective due to a recession in its product market; it may at the same time be efficient in the way it utilizes its resources.

2. Goals establish guidelines as to how an organization should function. They lay the foundations for the organization planning process. (See Chapter 7). In large, complex organizations goals tend to be arranged in a hierarchical fashion. The overall organization goal at the top of the hierarchy following by functional departmental and individual goals.
3. The establishment and communication of goals may act as a motivating device to members within the organization. As indicated in Chapter 4 individual behaviour tends to be goal directed.

Despite the central importance of goals to organization activity, behavioural scientists have pointed out a number of problems surrounding the identification of organization goals.

Problems of Goal Identification

The first problem associated with goal identification concerns the very question of whether organizations can be said to have any goals. Cyert and March (1963) have argued that organizations as abstract entities do not have goals, rather, it is groups and individuals within organizations who have goals. By endowing organizations with human characteristics, e.g. performing actions, taking decisions, having goals, we are in fact personifying organizations. As expanded upon later, Cyert and March conclude that organizations have multiple goals which result from the interaction of the major interest groups within them.

The second problem surrounding the identification of organization goals is distinguishing actual goals from stated goals. The two are not always synonymous. When organizations are established there is normally some formal written statement which expresses their goals. However, researchers observing organization behaviour question whether these goals are the major determining forces behind organization activity. Perrow (1961) describes these formal goals as 'official goals' whereas the goals which tend to influence actual behaviour in organizations are referred to as 'operative goals' which are linked directly to the numerous interest groups which make up the organization. Therefore, the study of organization effectiveness requires a close examination of these operative goals which may or may not be in line with the official goals.

Perrow's classification is similar to that which distinguishes goals as either ends in themselves (official goals) or means to achieving the ends (operative goals). When an organization's original goals (ends) are effectively substituted by other goals which normally represent the means to achieve the original ends, this is referred to as goal displacement. The result is a reversal of ends and means with the latter becoming the goals of the organization. The process of goal displacement was pointed out by Michels in 1911 in his study *Political Parties*, which examined socialist parties and trade unions in Western Europe. He argued that in those organizations the maintenance of the organization and the desire of the leadership to retain office became more important organization ends than the original goals set in accordance with socialist doctrines. By controlling the information and communication networks, officials were able to retain their positions, a situation Michels described as the 'iron law of oligarchy'.

Merton (1940) criticized the operation of bureaucratic organizations in a similar vein. He claimed that goal displacement could occur in bureaucracies when adherence to the well-defined rules and procedures of an organization became an end in itself rather than the means of attaining the goals of an organization.

A final point on goal identification is that goals are influenced by, and may change in response to, environmental pressures. Thompson and McEwen (1958) argued that organization goal-setting is influenced by four different forms of interaction with the environment:

1. Competition with other organizations, e.g. business organizations competing in product and labour markets.
2. Bargaining between organizations, e.g. collective bargaining between employers and trade unions.
3. Co-optation which involves external organizations being granted internal influence, e.g. banks providing board directors in business organizations.
4. Coalition formation between two or more organizations.

Behavioural scientists have pointed out some of the problems surrounding organization goals and it is against this background that we now turn to discuss the nature of goals in business organizations. The more complex analysis of organization goals by behavioural scientists contrasts with the early approaches of classical economists who, looking as business organizations, simply assumed profit maximization was the primary goal.

Nature of Business Organization Goals

Blau and Scott (1963) distinguish business organizations from other types of organization by identifying the owners as the primary beneficiaries. In addition to business concerns, they list three other categories of organizations:

1. Mutual benefit associations where the primary beneficiaries are the members, e.g. trade unions and political parties.
2. Service organizations, the primary beneficiaries, are the specific clients drawn from the general public, e.g. universities, hospitals.
3. Commonweal organizations where the primary beneficiaries are the general public, e.g. police force, postal services.

It should be noted that the 'primary beneficiary' approach to the classification of organizations is one of numerous typologies. For another alternative see Etzioni's approach at the end of this chapter. Parsons (1965) distinguishes four types of organizations on the basis of the function which they fulfill in society production, political, integrative and pattern maintenance organizations. Contingency theorists, however, consider these approaches unsatisfactory bases for the comparative analysis of organizations. They would argue that organizations may span more than one category and wide differences may occur within each category. As a result they concentrate on other characteristics. For example, as mentioned in Chapter 1, Burns and Stalker (1961) distinguish between mechanistic and organic organizations.

In discussing organization goals another common distinction is made between private and public sector organizations. Private sector organization fall within Blau and Scott's business concerns category while public sector organizations are more likely to be found in categories 2 and 3 above.

In public sector generally covers the organizations of central government (e.g. Department of Employment), local government (e.g. educational establishments) and public corporations (e.g. British Steel, National Coal Board). These organizations are usually established to meet some general social needs which governments consider cannot be supplied adequately on a normal free enterprise basis, e.g. defence, fire services. However, the ultimate extent of the public sector will depend on certain social and political choices as to whether or not certain goods or services should be supplied on a private enterprise or public sector basis, e.g. the extent of nationalized industries, the health service, utility services (gas, electricity). However, the arguments concerning this point lie beyond the scope of this book. It is considered that the objectives of public sector organizations are more ambiguous than private sector firms and are not directly linked to the profit motive. As the goals of these organizations are to meet social rather than economic criteria, measures of efficiency and effectiveness are more difficult to derive. Nationalized industries, similar to private sector firms, are often engaged in trading activities and it is easier to apply economic criteria to assess their performance. Goals are ultimately set by government guidelines and for nationalized industries these may include breaking even, obtaining a minimum rate of return on assets employed or even making profits.

If the goals of public sector organizations are considered ambiguous, the goals of private sector organizations have always been assumed to be linked to the profit motive. In contrasts to the private sector, the public sector is owned and financed by the State. In the private sector the owners who are the shareholders invest capital in order to reap returns in profits, paid as dividends. Hence Blau and Scott's classification of the primary beneficiaries of business concerns being owners. Note that different types of business concerns exist, e.g. sole proprietor, partnership, joint stock company. Such business concerns exist to satisfy consumer demands and if successful the owners are rewarded by profits. This raises the question of whether or not the sole goal of business organizations is, as classical economists assumed, the maximization of profits.

With the growth of large-scale, complex business organizations, it is now apparent that it is an over simplification to consider the goal of firms in singular profit maximization terms. The classical economic assumption of profit maximization implies that the interests of the firm's owners and managers are identical. This may have been more appropriate where the entrepreneur acted as owner manager but with the growth of large companies there has been a divorce of ownership and control. In modern companies shareholders as the owners of the company entrust the running of the affairs of the organization to a professional management team. Burnham (1941) in his book *Managerial Revolution* argued that control has passed to managers who pursued their own ambitions, which were not necessarily in line with profit maximization.

Alternative schools of thought on managerial goals have been developed.

1. Baumol (1967) argued that managers seek to maximize sales revenue since business success is perceived as being linked to the size of the market share which in turn may increase a manager's salary and promotion prospects. Profit is not irrelevant and manages are concerned with maximizing sales within minimum profit constraints, sufficient to keep shareholders satisfied.
2. Williamson's Management Discretion Theory (1967) argued in a similar vein to Baumol that managers had considerable freedom to pursue their own objectives as long as they achieved minimum profit levels. According to his theory, managers' needs were satisfied by their own salaries and 'perks', the number and quality of non-production staff they control, and the amount of discretionary investment power they possess.
3. Other writers emphasize the increasing responsibility of the business organization to the society in which they belong. Is the company a good citizen? Managerial decision-making is increasingly constrained by social obligations which are often reflected in government legislation. For example, consumers are afforded protection by the Sale of Goods Act (1979), employees' interests are safeguarded by the Employment Protection Consolidation Act (1978) while trading and commercial activities of companies are restricted by the various companies acts. Apart from legislation, the local community observes norms for companies and a manager may wish his company to be looked upon as a 'good company' e.g. in paying fair wages, or disposing of effluent without polluting the environment.
4. Managerial goals are no longer viewed in unidimensional terms but are often thought of as a combination of goals, e.g. growth in terms of sales, survival, long-term profitability and social responsibility. Galbraith in the *New Industrial State* (1967) argues than in western capitalist countries management have a number of goals which are given the following order of priority:

- The first priority is to ensure the survival and levels of profitability sufficient to satisfy shareholders and creditors.
- Once this is achieved the manager can seek to fulfill his own aspirations for greater power, status and prestige which motivates him to attain the second priority of seeking a higher rate of growth for the organization in terms of increased sales.
- Thirdly, mangers seek to improve their technological standing by creating new products, customers and jobs. And family, managers will take into account the social responsibilities of the organization.

5. A final contribution to the discussion of business organization goals is the Behavioural Theory developed by Cyert and March (1963) and mentioned earlier in this chapter. Cyert and March improve our understanding of why organizations sometimes have multiple goals and how these goals are determined. They argue that organizations do not have goals but that only individuals have goals. They view the organization as a coalition of individuals, many of whom belong to an interest group which has its own set of goals. Interest groups in the organization include not only the owners, managers and employees (internal coalition members) but also groups such as customers, suppliers, creditors, government and society in general (external coalition members). All interest groups may influence decision-making within the organization and are sometimes referred to as stakeholders.

Each interest group places constraints on managerial decision-making, e.g. customers' demand tastes, government legislation on restrictive practices, employees' desire to obtain favourable wages and conditions, owners' requirements for a satisfactory rate of return. As leaders of organizations, managers have to endeavour to satisfy to some degree the needs of the various interest groups. The presence of diverse interest groups will inevitably lead to goal conflict. Cyert and

March argue that the final goal set of the organization results from the political process of bargaining between interest groups and as their power may vary over time so may the multiple goals of organizations, e.g. increasing awareness of business organizations' social responsibilities has influenced company policies in the last decade. Note that although conflict is inevitable, in order for the organization to survive some goal compatibility must occur.

Business organizations may therefore be pursuing multiple goals rather than simply seeking to maximize profits. Simon (1967) suggests that it is unrealistic to assume that organizations maximize any goals during the decision-making process. In reaching decisions managers engage in satisfing behaviour rather than maximizing behaviour. The claims of various interest groups are often competitive and the complexity of the factors which management has to take into account prevents any maximizing behaviour.

Goal Conflict

It has already been stated that organizations, viewed as a coalition of interest groups, will experience organization conflict. Goal conflict may occur not only at the level of interest groups but also at the individual level. Clearly, individual goals in large, complex organizations may conflict with those of the organizations as a whole. Chapter 4 on Motivation indicates the types of need which employees wish to satisfy at work. Etzioni's (1961) classification of organizations recognizes that individual goals may conflict with stated organization goals. He therefore distinguishes between organizations according to the degree of commitment of the individual to the organization goals. In his analysis there are three types of organizations which correspond to the types of power used to elicit compliance with organization goals. These are as follows:

1. Coercive organizations, e.g. prisons, where members of the organization are negatively committed to organization goals and their involvement is described as alienative.

To achieve compliance, power is coercive based on the use or threat of physical sanctions.

2. Remunerative or utilitarian organizations, e.g. banks, manufacturing companies, where members of the organization have a low commitment to organization goals and their involvement is described as calculative. To achieve compliance, power is remunerative based on control over the allocation of rewards especially wages.
3. Normative organizations, e.g. churches, political parties where members' commitment to organization goals is high and their involvement is described as moral. To achieve compliance, normative power is usually based on moral persuasion.

Summary

- Though fundamental to an understanding of organizations, goal identification is not always easy. Behavioural scientists have questioned whether or not organizations can be said to have goals, pointed out that 'operative' goals may vary from 'official' goals, highlighted the phenomenon of goal displacement and indicated the important influence of the environment on goal-setting.
- It was concluded that a useful view of organization goals was provided by behavioural theory which emphasizes that business organizations often have multiple goals and are involved in satisfing behaviour rather than maximizing behaviour. Finally, the subject of goal conflict has been introduced and Etzioni's classification of organizations outlined.

Self-Learning Activity

Try to answer the following questions on your own:

1. How is organizational goal setting is influenced?
2. What do you understand by goal conflict?
3. Discuss alternative schools of thought on managerial goals.

9

Organization Control

If it is to fulfill its primary purpose the organization requires more than mere identification of its goals. Some means of attainment must be provided, and, if the organization is to stay on course, this process needs to be controlled in some way. Control implies regulation, that is to say, activities must be of such a nature that they meet organization goals. In this sense we are talking about formal goals and mechanisms which enable formal control. Systems of control enable the organization to monitor its activities and take corrective action where required, in order that its objectives may be met. The organization will want to identify its failings and establish why they have occurred. Any attempt to carryout this process represents control, enabling re-adjustment whereby objectives can reflect more accurately organization strategy.

Control–Some Considerations

Control is also important because it enables the organization to function in a manner which creates the necessary degree of co-ordination. The sheer complexity of many organization processes— administrative and technical, demand the use of control procedures if they are to function effectively. There are various ways of achieving co-ordination and the use of particular control mechanisms will depend on the nature of the organization's objectives, its organization and management structures, technology and its cultural norms.

Control would be simplified if it could be assumed that everyone within the organization had similar objectives, or that its various processes were self-regulating. In practice this does not occur. In the case of the former, individual motives, objectives and behaviour have to be considered as much a reality of organization life as those which are counted part of the organization's formal goals. The individual represents his own unique position within the overall hierarchy of organization membership and is influenced by his own ambitions and perceptions surrounding his role. He is also affected by events and experiences outside the workplace and these may condition his response to the work situation. We cannot even assume that management in its corporate sense always acts in such a way as to suggest a unified view of organization objectives. The individual manager may view his specific departmental objectives as being more important or significant than some more generally stated overall objectives. He may feel that the former serve his own ends more adequately in that they are felt to be more pertinent to the realization of his own goals. Actions taken by the individual manager do not always reflect the total mission particularly when the matter may involve questions of status and power.

Control Methods

When considering the various methods of organization control we can distinguish between:

1. The use of formal authority.
2. Control through standardization.

Use of formal authority this has its origins in classical organization theory, and in bureaucracy in particular, and is based on the notion of voluntary acceptance of legitimate authority, and therefore of orders, directives, and requests. In practice this entails supervision achieved through the application of principles relating to identification of authority at each level of the organization, and the establishment of a chain of command and spans of control. Thus, one level of office carries with it authority and responsibility over the one beneath it. Often, the exercise of this form of control will involve the manager in directing, assessing and correcting actions related to his subordinate's work performance and general behaviour. In turn he will be subject to the same process by his superior, and so on up the chain of command. In the business organization legitimacy arises out of the office or level of job rather than as a factor relating to the personality of the job-holder. This provides the organization with some stability, even when it is faced with sudden changes in staff, and helps to minimize disruption to the process of meeting objectives.

In large and complex organizations this process of control can be complicated by the existence of a number of chains of command affecting the role of the individual. A subordinate may be required to report to two different supervisors for different aspect of his job. If control involving the use of formal authority is to be effective, careful consideration needs to be given to ensure that the division of task content, responsibility and reporting relationships are fully understood by both supervisors and subordinates.

Formal authority as a means of control exists in another sense which does not rest on the superior authority inherent in one job as compared to another, but arises because managerial jobs at the different levels of the organization carry with them certain requirements and rights relating to access, consultation and negotiation with others in the management hierarchy, particularly those in peer relationships. Lateral communications of this nature may be necessary to the successful discharge of responsibility and serve as a means of control by establishing a system of checks and balances. For example, the marketing manager in an organization may need to liaise with and advise the sales manager. One does not necessarily have right of supervision over the other, but the process of consultation which ensues may serve as an important restraint on either manager doing exactly as he pleases regardless of any other consideration. Each person in this type of transaction is recognizing authority in the other's role and may modify his own preferences in favour of reaching agreement.

Control through standardization may take a number of different forms. The existence of rules and procedures to which reference can be made prior to reaching decisions is an important example. These have the effect of placing limits on the discretion of individual managers thus removing the likelihood of embarrassing precedents being created. For instance, two managers within the same organization but operating in different departments and possibly in different physical locations may each be faced with a similar problem. Each manager, independently of the other, may investigate and analyse the problem and then apply the appropriate rule or procedure to the solution of his problem. Both problems and solutions are similar, and thus, consistency of treatment is assured, enabling stability. The existence of rules and procedures also provides employees with the opportunity to develop their understanding of the processes whereby problems are dealt with. The employee may feel that consistency in treatment provides a more equitable basis than decisions based on one individual's interpretation of events or facts. This is likely to be of particular importance where the problem is concerned with some aspect of labour management.

However, this approach to management control has its weaknesses in that too great a dependency on rules and procedures is likely to lead to a loss of management discretion. The rule or procedure may come to be seen as being more important in itself than the problem to which it is being applied. In situations where this is carried to excess, allegations associated with some of the disadvantages of bureaucracy are likely to arise, notably that the means to the ends have became more important than the ends themselves. In practice it is difficult to provide a rule or procedure which will cover precisely every problem that is likely to be encountered. Employees, while respecting consistency, may nevertheless eventually become hostile to a control system which does not permit variations in treatment according to the specific situation under consideration. Moves towards organization decentralization, with its emphasis on less mechanistic structure, make control of this sort less appropriate. Flexibility in the handling of problems is becoming increasingly important in the face of a noticeable decline in the efficacy of traditional formal authority. Many managerial jobs require exercise of a considerable measure of discretion if they are to be considered effective.

Overall, excessive emphasis on the use of formal authority, whether of a direct supervisory nature of through the application of rules and procedures, is likely to provoke reaction on the part of the employee and encourage the development of attitudes and behaviour which will result in jobs being performed at minimum standard. Motivation may be poor and the individual's realization of making a useful and meaningful contribution will be low. Co-operation and creativity may well be lost to the organization as a result.

Control through standardization also takes another form where work methods are standardized in such a way as to ensure consistency in manufacturing processes and thus in the product. This form of control can be applied at the level of the department, the work group or the individual. An example which illustrates this is to be found in connection with the system of production in a manufacturing company. The system will comprise input, transformation and output stages. Methods of control can be applied to any or all of these stages.

Work standardization has become particularly important in manufacturing industry. In part it removes the need for constant direct supervision, replacing it with an authority based on the design, planning and implementation of technical standards, adherence to which provides the required degree of control. In effect, technical authority is more relevant to the needs of the organization than formal management authority exercised through direction. Here, we have used the production process as our example but standardization is often used to control the work of other functions. Financial control through the establishment of budgets and monitoring of costs is one such example. Management training aimed at standardizing behaviour is yet another.

Control and Planning

Associated with control is the process of planning. Planning involves all levels of the organization even though its impetus may stem from top management. Corporate planning requires identification of the company's overall strategy and the range of measures needed to be taken to enable realization. The translation of strategy into a series of plans eventually results in the setting of functional, departmental and individual objectives. However, before this stage is attained the strategy itself must be determined. Primarily, this arises through an examination of both external and internal environments. For example, assessment of the external environment is likely to include market opportunity, the state of technology, government policy and availability of capital and labour. Assessment of the internal environment requires the organization to take a considered view of its strengths and weaknesses in relation to existing resources, competence and so on. Both processes will create information which may then be used to determine business objectives and appropriate product development and manufacture. Generally, the questions needed to be asked include:

1. What position is the organization in at the present time?
2. What are its objectives for the future?
3. What will constitute an acceptable level of profits?
4. What are its social responsibilities?

The process of translating strategy into plans for all levels of the organization, determining priorities, ensuring that plans incorporate desired objectives, monitoring performance in the meeting of objectives, all illustrate the presence of control. As plans are broken down into objectives they usually become more detailed, and at lower levels may appear as little more than a set of instructions with limited or no discretion rather than as a statement of objectives. In effect chain and unity of command principles are being employed so that objectives met at one level help to fulfill objectives at the next level above and so on until the plans are realized, and the organization's strategy is eventually discharged.

Clearly, successful control will be subject to the adequacy of organization strategy. For example if, initially, the organization places the wrong interpretation on what is happening in the environment, then however successful the ensuring control process is, it will not compensate for the strategy having been poorly founded. Likewise, translation of the planning process from initial strategy to final objectives and to more specific goals must be competently handled, otherwise an adequate strategy will founder due to imperfections in the control process. There are many pitfalls awaiting unwary managements!

Complex technology and circumstances surrounding projects provide further example of the need for and use of planning. Here the problem is to control the many activities or events which contribute to a project in such a way as to make the best use of money, manpower, time and other resources. One means of establishing control is to use a technique such as Project Evaluation and Review Technique (PERT). This is a planning technique using network diagrams. Typically, it is used in project where many different activities are involved, and where it is difficult to identify the amount of time taken by each activity. It aims to predict the likelihood of attaining each stage or event of the project by identified target dates, and is based on the use of statistical techniques, notably probability. A three time estimate of each activity ranging through optimistic, most likely, to pessimistic is usually employed. Each activity is indicated by arrows which represent the order in which it is undertaken. At the points at which arrows meet, numbers are ascribed which identify events in the life of the project. These form the basis of the network.

A further network planning system commonly found is that of critical path analysis. This technique is also widely used in projects and is related to identification of the duration of the project giving minimum cost. It is used primarily to estimate the cost and time period of each activity. Unlike PERT it normally employs on estimate based on overage time related to completion of an activity.

If control is to be effective, adequate feedback must be provided. Information concerned with performance requires monitoring, analysis and assessment by successively higher levels of management before any further decisions are taken.

Feedback also exists as an important component of the monitoring process in situations in which formal authority is being exercised. In this instance it is reaction to the outcome of particular decisions which provides the feedback in other words, the consequences of that decision in the form of information. Are the consequence the expected ones or by their very nature could they not have been anticipated? What effect will this have on future decisions if and when a similar problem arises? Similar considerations apply to the application of formal rules and procedures, and the extent to which consequences resulting from the implementation of a rule or procedure reinforce management's belief in the validity of the latter or bring about the desire for change. The existence of management information systems provides a further example of feedback and the proliferation of reports arising from different parts of the organization owes much to the requirement for generating information. Basically, feedback services to remind us of the dynamic and ongoing nature of organization life, where strategy, plans, objectives and goals are subjects to constant reformulation. It represents an essential link between the process of communication; without feedback adequate control would be impossible.

Management By Objectives

A major feature of traditional authority systems is that they are imposed by managers or by the organization, and thereby reflect particular values. Essentially, they provide a process whereby participation on the part of the subordinate is minimized. The individual is expected either to respond to the control in a manner favourable to the meeting of formal objectives of suffer the consequences. However, in practice employee may find some way of rejecting the imposition of authority, for example, by withdrawing cooperation. McGregor has drawn our attention to the assumptions underlying management's traditional viewpoint and practice in the exercise of control. McGregor's proportions identify the nature of the management task as being one of persuading, rewarding, punishing and controlling the workforce in order to get tasks accomplished. It is suggested that this approach stems from a belief that man is by nature lazy and that he will exert himself as little as possible, that he dislikes responsibility, is self-centred and resistant to change. Reacting resulting from management practice based on this viewpoint may be treated simply by administering more of the same does, that is by tightening control even further.

However, alternative approaches are possible and one of the best known is that of Management By Objectives (M.B.O). The essential feature here involves a process of establishing job objectives based on mutual agreement between a manager and subordinate. One aspect of this approach is that a system of staff appraisal, based on performance factors related directly to the job, is frequently employed. It is claimed that a subordinate's involvement becomes more substantial and a situation is created in which he will work harder and more effectively. Because he has been encouraged to be the mainspring of his own objectives his attitudes and behaviour will demonstrate greater commitment to the overall goals of the organization. Faced with inevitable hierarchical structures, organizations are concerned to make them work effectively. This entails control, but M.B.O. attempts to provide an approach which increases the likelihood of achieving teamwork based on mutual consensus as regards goals, and identification of what is expected of the individual. Both manager and subordinate will understand the level of job performance which is expected and will be working within a clearly defined framework. Consequently the possibility of uncertainty surrounding both individual and organization objectives will be removed and, if the process is implemented throughout, should result in the development of a more supportive climate which will enhance the quality of relationships within an organization.

It is also claimed that high levels of involvement on the part of employees will assist the process of evaluating performance. M.B.O. requires a measures of self-appraisal on the part of the individual and there is some evidence to suggest that weaknesses are viewed more objectively, possibly because a greater feeling of security exists; in turn this may enable a situation where corrective action is more acceptable. Furthermore, emphasis on the achievement of results may remove some of the doubts surrounding traditional staff appraisal because there is less opportunity for subjectivity to creep into assessments. It is actual achievement which is emphasized. M.B.O. is intended to appeal to the individual's desire for involvement, creativity and autonomy. As with other form of control, M.B.O. makes assumptions about the nature of the relationship between the individual and his job. McGregor's Theory Y (See Chapter 4) provides some insights into the basis of such assumptions. It proposes a view of man which suggests that he possesses potential for development, is not inherently lazy and will not shirk responsibility and that what is needed is a management approach that encourages the emergence of more positive human characteristics. McGregor further proposes:

1. That the essential task of management is to arrange organization conditions and methods of operation so that people can achieve their own goals best by directing their own efforts toward organization objectives.
2. This is a process primarily of creating opportunities, releasing potential, removing obstacles, encouraging growth, and providing guidance.

McGregor's Theory may offer a more realistic interpretation of the needs of individuals working in modern complex organizations, and raises the possibility of creating a more holistic attitude towards the formal objectives of the business. Its ideas are suggestive of a unitary view, and are worthy of consideration even when they are not expressed in the context of a formal M.B.O. programme.

Problems can arise with Theory Y because its assumptions about human motivation imply a general theory approach which cannot be supported on the basis of existing evidence. Some people are motivated in the manner desired while others, victims perhaps of more traditional approaches to the exercise of control, cannot wholly remove suspicion from their minds that M.B.O. still represents authoritarianism albeit in a disguised form and is really a form of pseudo participation. Opponents of M.B.O. argue that despite its claims, it does not overcome the reward/punishment psychology underlying hierarchical relationships: the implied threat continues to be present ready to be invoked in the case of failure. They question the reality surrounding the involvement of the subordinate in the objective setting process, arguing that actual choice of goals is in fact limited by the manager who will continue to be the final arbiter of what is allowable. A further problem is that over-dependence on the use of job descriptions may result in too narrow a view on what constitutes acceptable objectives. For example, there are some aspects of a manager's job which are difficult to describe meaningfully, let alone quantity as part of the objective setting process. Relationships with other managers may comprise an important dimension and influence how well the individual manager performs, and yet this may be overlooked in the quest for measurable data.

However, whatever the drawbacks with M.B.O., it is likely that organizations will continue to seek control mechanisms which encourage participation and create a climate where the need for control is given genuine recognition by all.

Increasingly, participation will become the key in establishing forms of control which enable both organizations and individuals to achieve goal satisfaction with a minimum of conflict.

Informal Relationships

The discussions so far have centered on formal control related to formal organization objectives. However, it is necessary to make some comment on the existence of informal relationships and the extent to which they comprise a form of control system. The Human Relations View of the informal organization tends to focus on the organization itself as an identifiable entry with its own social structure, communication and status systems. However, more recent studies, notably Silverman's *Theory of Organizations* (1970), suggest that this separatist is not a wholly accurate reflection of how the total system works, and that formal and informal organizations are really interdependent. Undoubtedly, we can point to the existence of informal communication networks which reflect information flow based on mutual interests and a desire to see those interests realized. Such networks embrace personnel at all levels of the organization, including managers, and supplement communication flows arising out of formal channels of control. They enable the organization to function, as well as reflecting the social nature of life within the organization. In practice, the informal channels provide links between those with shared interests and thus enable powerful pressure groups to be formed.

Formal control systems have to exist alongside pressure groups and acknowledge their existence. Constant readjustment based on the dual processes of negotiation and consultation is likely to be demanded, and can assist the organization to maintain its health and stability. Conflict is most likely to occur when the existence of informal channels and the role they play are denied. Their existence reflects more accurately the day-to-day circumstances of organization life and is in keeping with Fox's view that the organization is a 'coalition of interests'.

Summary

- Control implies regulation, that is to say, activities must be of such a nature that they meet organization goals. In this sense we are talking about formal goals and mechanisms which enable formal control.
- Systems of control enable the organization to monitor its activities and take corrective action where required, in order that its objectives may be met.
- Formal control systems have to exist alongside pressure groups and acknowledge their existence.

Self-Learning Activity

Try to answer the following questions on your own:

1. How can you distinguish while considering various methods of organization control?
2. Describe MBO.

10

Influence, Power, Authority, Leadership

The discussion of goals in Chapter 8 reference to the fact that individuals have goals which are not always in line with those of the organization. Chapter 4 demonstrated how people possessing a similar ability level may perform differently due to motivational factors and examined what motivates people (content theories) and how people are motivated (process theories). Based on this understanding of the complexity of individual motivation, managers, acting as leaders, have to motive employees so that they channel their efforts into pursuing organization goals. Leadership forms the bridge between organization goals and individual goals and is a crucial element in determining the success of the organization. It is the process by which managers influence the behaviour and attitudes of subordinates.

How can managers become more effective leaders? The answer to this question is important to organizations seeking to improve their performance and also has implications for the selection and training of managers. Before attempting to answer this question, the first part of this chapter will look at authority, power and influence in organizations, all of which are inextricably linked to the leadership process. The effectiveness of leadership, as shall be seen later, is related in part to the leader's power base.

Influence, Power and Authority in Organizations

Human relations in organizations are concerned with the interaction of individuals and groups, and behind this interaction usually lies power and influence as the efforts of employees are steered towards the goals of the organization. Many writers have stated that fundamental to an understanding of behaviour in organizations is an understanding of the nature of influence, power and authority. What then are influence, power and authority?

Influence is where A (the influencer) changes the attitudes or behaviour of B (the influence). Power is interpreted as the capability to exercise influence over the behaviour of others and is often defined in Dahl's (1957) terms as being something A has over B, to the extent that A can get B to act in a certain way, in which B may not have acted but for the power that A had over B. The more power individuals or groups have, the more successful they are likely to be in influencing the attitudes and behaviour of other individuals and groups. Though closely associated with power, authority is distinguished as the right to influence and is equivalent to legitimate power.

Most organizations are of a hierarchical nature and the chain of command is downwards through the hierarchy. At different levels in the hierarchy, authority will be exercised by someone performing a role, e.g. a foreman, a works manager. The degree of influence attached to a role will depend on its level in the hierarchy the higher the level the greater the degree of influence. The authority or right to issue commands is viewed as legitimate because it is accepted by the members of the organization as residing in the position the person in authority occupies in the hierarchy. Weber called this kind of authority rational-legal authority. He also identified two other types of authority, charismatic authority, which is respected by organization members because of the person's qualities, and traditional authority, which results from well established methods of operating within the organization.

Rational-legal authority is dependent upon and organization's acceptance of its legitimacy but in the post-war period most industrially developed countries have experienced major challenges to legitimate authority in many of their major institutions. Rising education levels and higher standards of living have contributed to higher expectations concerning work, with employees wanting greater influence over the decisions taken in organizations to which they belong. The major challenge to managerial authority has come from trade unions, who have sought to reduce the decision-making areas over which management has sole control. (The unilateral rights of management to make rules which influence the employment relationship is sometimes referred to as managerial prerogative.) As a result there has been an extension in the scope of collective bargaining and joint consultation, increasing demands for more interesting work and for employee representation on boards of directors.

A number of countries in Western Europe already have some form of employee representation on company boards of directors, for example, the West German co-determination system. The EEC legal harmonization programme is likely to extend board representation regulations to all member states. In U.K. the public sector has initiated a number of experiments: for example, since 1968 the British Steel Corporation has had worker directors on its divisional boards.

One area in which the scope of collective bargaining has recently been increased is in the field of technological change. For example, the microprocessor has revolutionized office equipment by introducing machines like word processors. In a number of companies management, seeking the smooth introduction of such equipment, has jointly negotiated technology agreements with its trade union representatives. These agreements cover items such as the procedural issues surrounding change (e.g. when union representatives should be consulted, disclosure of information), job security, the distribution of the benefits of introducing new technology (e.g., wages, hours, holidays) and problems related to operating the equipment (e.g., health-related problems associated with visual display units, like eye strain).

The process of collective bargaining itself is a power relationship between organized labour and management and illustrates that power is not exclusively in the hands of management. It is a process which seeks to resolve the conflict of interest which may exist between the management and the workforce. Where management has recognized trade unions as being a legitimate interest group within the organization, trade unions in turn have recognized the legitimacy of management to manage within the agreed constraints established by collective bargaining.

The 'manager's right to manage' is likely to be challenged further in the future. As well as being constrained by workers' organizations, managerial authority is increasingly restricted by legislation introduced by governments, for example, unfair dismissal rights, social responsibilities in terms of the environment.

The above discussion has briefly explored the challenges to managerial authority which may be equated with legitimate power. However, other sources of power may be open to managers and an examination of these alternatives helps us to understand how individuals are capable of influencing other people. French and Raven (1959) identified five bases of individual power. Taking A as the influencer and B as the influences, these are as follows:

1. *Position power or legitimate power:* This is the power which is based upon the formal rights and duties attached to a role in the organization hierarchy. The influence of A is considered legitimate and is accepted by B. The rights of the role include the right to information which may come from above or below of that organization level, the right of access to organization decision-making bodies, for example, committees, and the right to organize work activities. With this power source, individuals tend to

influence other individuals or groups by rules and procedures which may restrict individual freedom or maintain the status quo. For these rules and procedures to have the desired effect on B, A's right to make the rules and procedures must be accepted by B and A must normally have the resources power to backup his position power; this leads on the second major power base.

2. *Resource power or reward power:* The validity of position power normally requires the backup of resource power which is the control A has over rewards to B. To be effective B must obviously value the rewards which A has under his control. The most obvious rewards over which A has control and B values are financial rewards, for example, pay and fringe benefits. However, rewards may not just be financial and may include status and recognition. Resource power is usually mediated via exchange or bargaining methods where A give B something for behaving in the way A requires. The effort-bargain relationship common to pay bargaining agreements, especially where payment by results schemes operate, is a good example of this method of influence in that workers will exert an amount of effort in return for certain financial rewards.

3. *Coercive power:* This is also closely related to resource power and is the power to decide not to reward and to punish non-obedience: the ability of A to punish B. Punishment in industrial organizations is not, of course, of a physical nature, but can, for example, include such measures as demotion, withholding salary increases, transfer to other work and dismissal. The method of influence implied is one of force, though again in industrial organizations this is rarely, if ever, physical force. However, in the collective bargaining relationship a coercive approach to persuade the other side to agree to your offer or claim may entail the use of economic force, where each side has the power to inflict economic

damage on their opponent. A strike or lockout would involve the loss of wages to individual workers and the loss of company profits.

4. *Expert power:* Challenges to managerial authority have tended to be directed towards the previous three source of power, whereas the remaining power bases appear to be more acceptable. Expert power stems from A having the knowledge and skill in an area which B does not possess; therefore in this area B is willing to accept A's influence. A can usually obtain B's compliance by persuasion. Expert power in areas which are crucial to the attainment of organization success may give the powerholder an important organization role with its associated position power source. So, if A's expertise is questioned it may be possible for A to resort to the methods associated with position power or resource power. The level of expert power exercised will be related to the degree to which A can be substituted. If A is difficult to replace he is likely to be in a very strong position.
5. *Personal power or referent power:* This is similar to Weber's charismatic authority type. A's power stems from his personal attributes and B will accept A's influence because he admires him. A may try to influence B through persuasion, which is facilitated by personal power, but often the charisma of A alone will be sufficient to get B to alter his behaviour. It is worth noting that the method of persuasion can be used with any power source and though time consuming it is normally a very acceptable method individuals feel they are doing something for the powerholder to which they have voluntarily given their consent.

LEADERSHIP

Definition

Dubin R. defines: "Leadership is the exercise of authority and making of decisions".

G.R. Terry defines: "Leadership is the activity of influencing people to strive willingly for group objectives".

Goals of Leadership

A leader should keep the following goals:

Organisational Goals

These are formal goals laid down by the organisation, which have to be achieved by the leader.

Group Goals

These are the informal goals, which evolve through the interaction of members of the group.

Follower's Personal Goals

This refers to what the subordinate look for in his job, such as a sense of security.

Leader's Personal Goals

This reflects the goals or personal ends desired to be achieved by the leader.

Characteristics of Leadership

Presupposes following

Without followers there can be no leaders. So all leaders should have good number of followers.

Working Relationships

A leader shows the way by being in the forefront and asks his men to follow him. He takes people along with him.

Exemplary Conduct

By keeping good conduct a leader becomes an example to his followers. What he is judged by what he does and how he behaves.

Community of Interest

There must be community of interest between the leader and his men. Both must have common purpose to achieve.

Problem-solving Skill

A leader should have the ability to solve problems.

Some theories of leadership are discussed below:

1. TRAIT THEORY

The trait theory emphasizes that leaders are born and not made. The traits are inherent personal qualities. This theory assumes that leadership is function of these traits. Some of the traits include intelligence, understanding, perception, high motivation, socio-economic status, initiative, maturity, need for self-actualisation, self-assurance and understanding of interpersonal human relations. The existence of these traits became a measure of leadership. It holds that the possession of certain traits permits certain individuals to gain positions of leadership.

Leadership implies activity movement and getting the work done. The leader is a person who occupies a position of responsibility in coordinating the activities of the members of a group. Hence, it is not possession of some traits but a pattern of personal characteristics bearing a relevant relationship to the goal of the followers, that makes a leader. The leadership must be conceived in terms of interactions-for one to lead and for others who want to be led.

The trait theory of leadership suffer from lack of conclusiveness and over simplification. The critics have charged that the theory focuses attention only on the leaders and disregards the dynamics of the leadership process. Also the theory ignores the situational characteristics which may result in emergence of a leader. Some of the other weaknesses and failures of the trait theory are:

(i) All the traits are not identical with regard to the essential characteristics of a leader.

(ii) Some traits can be acquired by training and may not be inherited.

(iii) The traits required to attain leadership may not be same that are required to sustain leadership.

(iv) It fails to explain the many leadership failures in spite of the required traits.

(v) It ignores the environmental factors which may differ from situation to situation.

2. BEHAVIOUR THEORY

This theory studies leadership by looking leaders in terms of what they do. The leader's effectiveness is judged in terms of individual subordinate outcome or work group outcome. Considerable investigations into this approach have been conducted at OhIO State University These studies isolated two particular factors affecting the leadership dimension. These are:

(a) Consideration connotes support between the leader and the group, a mutual warmth and trust, a concern for the needs of the members of the work group and attitudes that encourages a participative management, two-way communication and respect for the feedback of the followers.

(b) *Initiating structure:* This involves creating a work environment, so that the work of the group is organised, coordinates sequential, organisationally relevant, so that people know exactly what is to be done and how it is to be done. Structure involves having the leader organise and define the role each member is to assume, assign tasks and push for the realization of organisational goal. An Important discovery made by the Ohio studies was that the leader does not necessarily have to rate high both on consideration and structure element. He could be high on one and low on the other.

3. CONTINGENCY THEORY

This theory states, that an analysis of leadership involves the individual traits and behaviour. The leadership is used in combination with work group contingencies to predict outcomes. The effectiveness of the leader behaviour is contingent upon the demands imposed by the situation. There are three major components that are significant for leadership effectiveness. These include individual differences among leaders, difference among situations and the manner in which these two variables are related.

4. THE PATH-GOAL THEORY

The Path-Goal model of leadership behaviour has been profounded by Robert J. House. This model emphasises that the leader behaviour be such as to complement the group work setting. He sets up clear path and clear guidelines through which the subordinates can achieve both personal and work-related goals and assist them in achieving these goals. This will make the leader behaviour acceptable and satisfying to subordinates since they see the behaviour as an immediate source of satisfaction or as a source of obtaining future satisfaction. This approach is largely derived from the Path-Goal approach to motivation. To motivate the workers the leaders should:

(a) Recognise the subordinate's needs.

(b) Arrange for appropriate rewards to his followers for goal achievement.

(c) Helping subordinates is clearly establishing their expectations.

(d) Demolish as far as possible the barriers in their path of goal achievement.

(e) Increase opportunities for personal satisfaction which are contingent upon satisfactory performance.

There are four basic leadership styles that would support this approach depending upon the nature of situation.

(a) Directive Leadership

When the demands of a task on hand are ambiguous, directive leadership is needed. But when the task is inherently clean or clarification is otherwise available, then a high level of directive leadership may impede effective performance.

(b) *Supportive Leadership*

Supportive leadership is friendly and approachable and has the most positive effect on the satisfaction of followers working on unpleasant, stressful or frustrating tasks or tasks that are highly repetitive.

(c) *Achievement-oriented Leadership*

This type of performance standards increases confidence in their ability to meet challenging goals. This is specially true for followers who have clear-cut, non-repetitive assignments.

(d) *Participative Leadership*

This leadership style encourages subordinate's participation in the decision-making process. The leadership solicits subordinates suggestions and takes these suggestions seriously into consideration before making decisions.

5. VROOM-YETTON MODEL

This is a normative theory for it tells the leaders how they should behave in decision-making. The focus is on the premise that different problems have different characteristics and should, therefore, be solved by different decision techniques. The effectiveness of the decision is a function of leadership which ranges from the leader making the decisions himself to a totally democratic process in which the subordinates fully participate and the contingencies which describe the attributes of the problem to be dealt with. For a successful leader it is imperative to know the best approach to solving the problem at hand, and to know how to implement each decision-making method well, when required.

This model dictates that the decision reached should be high in quality, should be accepted by the people who have to implement it and should be time efficient. The leader while choosing a strategy decides which element he will focus on and which may be neglected to some extent. Studies performed to test the validity of this theory concluded that the participative and democratic style of leadership was more appropriate and successful at higher levels of an organization, whereas directive decision-making styles were utilized at lower levels.

Summary

- Having defined the purpose of leadership in terms of influencing the behaviour and attitude of other people the effectiveness of a leader must depend to some extent on power.
- The leader has to understand his sources of power and the methods of influence he can utilize. It is also important to realize that within organizations numerous individuals and groups have some modicum of power, if not quite considerable power.
- Power therefore is relative and the amount of successful influence, an individual may have, will depend on how far the balance of power is 'tilted' in his favour. In a similar vein the manager may not be the only leader in the organization; for example, leaders emerge from work groups, trade unionists elect shop stewards.
- Etzioni (1964) makes a useful distinction between formal and informal leaders. An informal leader controls others by using mainly personal power. A formal leader controls others by using both position power and personal power and it is within this category that managers fall.

Self-Learning Activity

Try to answer the following questions on your own:

1. What is the nature of influence, power and authority?
2. Explain Trait Theory of leadership.
3. Describe Vroom-Yetton Model of leadership.

11

Organization Conflict

Conflict is a reality of organization life. What is it and why does it occur? Conflict describes situations in which individuals and/or groups of people are in disagreement with each other with the result that inefficiencies or ineffectiveness occur. The scale of inefficiency may range from minimal interference to business operations through to the occurrence of serious dysfunctions. In the past, management's view of the cause of conflict has been simplistic, encouraged by the perspective offered by classical organization theory and related largely to the breakdown of formal authority and the need for measures which will restore it. In this light (management has seen the occurrence of conflict as rejection of its prerogative to govern and control. Thus, conflict is identified as deviant bahaviour and, therefore, is likely to incur punishment in one form or another. In practice this has meant a further tightening of control in order to attempt to minimize the likelihood of deviant behaviour occurring again). This situation suggests:

Management's expectations are based on a unitary view which carries with it the expectation that everyone within the organization has the same objectives, will work together as a team, acknowledge the legitimacy of hierarchical differences and respect superior authority. Anything which appears to interfere with this view is regarded as 'bad' behaviour and is dealt with according to rules, procedures, custom and conventions which exist within the particular organization. This view acknowledges the existence of 'management logic' but ignores the existence of other views on what constitutes rational response.

Management's view of conflict does not encompass the possibility of other causes. For example, Taylor saw conflict occurring either because of misunderstanding on the part of the worker as to his role, or because his, Taylor's, philosophy had not been properly applied.

If management's view is as narrow as suggested, then it is unlikely that sources of conflict other than infringement of formal authority will be identified and given genuine recognition. Any manifestation of conflict will be liable to be viewed and treated on the basis of breakdown of formal authority. Inevitably this means a lack of understanding of the many and varied sources of conflict, and suggests a situation in which management's competence to deal with conflict is limited. Adequate understanding and analysis of problems is a prerequisite of a successful treatment of conflict. If this is not forthcoming, ineffectiveness will result.

Causes of Conflict

We can identify possible causes of conflict as follows:

1. Differences between corporate and individual goals.
2. Conflicts between different departments or groups within the organization.
3. Conflict between formal and informal organization.
4. Conflict between manager and managed.
5. Conflict between individual and job.
6. Conflict between individuals.

Differences between Corporate and Individual Goals

Corporate goals relate to the organization as a total entity. This does not mean that each individual in the organization will subscribe to the same goals. Each individual has his own set of goals not all of which relate to the organization, although the latter may well serve as the means whereby some at least are satisfied. Differences in goal identification and goal-seeking pose the possibility of conflict. A further consideration is that individuals often fulfill different roles in several organizations simultaneously, and where organization goals differ and/or clash this may enhance the possibility of conflict. Attitudes and commitment towards organization goals may also depend on a member's position in the hierarchy. Those who are placed at the lower end of the scale may find it difficult to identify with goals to which higher management subscribes. Perceptions of what is desirable may differ between people at different levels and these may be reinforced by notions of status and realities of organization life. In many instances, individuals may well see the organization simply as a means of utility, often economic, which enables the satisfaction of goals related to life outside the organization. In management's eyes individuals may not represent the desired model of organization man — the extent of their commitment being reflected by the views they have of the organization's role in meeting their desire for economic or social utility.

Conflicts between Different Departments or Groups within the Organization

Reference to a corporate goal may be suggestive of a unitary view at least among those who hold positions of major authority and responsibility. However, an organization consists of function and department built around the requirements of specialization and each unit may develop a unique view of its objectives and status within the overall framework. Different departments and groups may have quite different interests and goals. Some will be concerned with maintaining the efficiency of the existing system and their views may be primarily inward-looking. Management services are an example. Others will perform a more adaptive role — the marketing function, for instance, which is primarily outward-looking. Each will identify priorities according to the nature of its perspective. A further form of conflict can exist between line and staff departments. As organizations grow and develop, they are subject to increasing specialization of function and task. As mentioned in Chapter 2, strong staff hierarchies may develop and encroach on what has previously been line management's authority. A staff function may be concerned with creating a system embodying various rules and procedures. By doing this it is attempting to engender conformity of action by those functions and departments which use its services. However, these other functions, particularly if they are line, may resent attempts to impose authority in this way and to place, what some may consider, restraints on freedom of action. They may find working within the system irksome, particularly where the rules emanate from a function or department to which they accord little respect and whose actions may be seen as interference, rather than the exercise of legitimate authority. Line personnel may seek to overrule the system by exercising their own initiative in dealing with problems, thus creating the possibility of inconsistencies and increasing the likelihood of conflict. A further example of conflict between groups is where they are competing for similar roles within the organization. In practice, competition of this sort often lends to focus on certain aspects of functional roles. For instance, the personnel function may have overall control over staff selection policy but line departments may also want to make actual selection decision in relation to individual appointments. In effect, we have a number of subsystems and the corporate goal is the outcome of argument, disagreement and conflict settled by negotiation, consultation and, at times, imposition of authority by higher levels in the hierarchy. At times groups may be operating under different frameworks of reference and this can also lead to conflict. This type of conflict may occur at the same level within the organization. One instance is where two or more groups of employees are competing for similar rewards. An example is pay, where conflict cannot be viewed as arising only out of differences between employers and employees, but also between employees themselves who may frequently argue and disagree over wage differentials.

Demarcation issues offer a further example where workers, anxious to preserve their own security of employment, battle over what to the outsider may seem trivial differences, but which for those involved comprise issues of considerable magnitude, with many implications.

Conflict between Formal and Informal Organization

This may arise because the formal organization has failed to satisfy some of the needs of individuals who then seek some alternative means of attaining their own goals. The informal system with its own status, communication and control mechanisms may be the means whereby individuals seek satisfaction. In formal goals and their process of attainment may be viewed as being undesirable by the formal organization which may try either to ignore such a process or seek activity to suppress it. Thus, conflict is generated by the pressures which arise when two groups compete in order to achieve a favourable outcome.

Conflict between Manager and Managed

This form is usually described and analysed under the heading of industrial relations and largely involves disputes over matters such as pay and working conditions. However, such disputes may also occur because those being managed want to be involved in decision-making processes likely to affect them, namely participation. This view represents a challenge to the traditional-exercise of authority by management, and may be indicative of attempts to create a wider power base and to lessen the imposition of authority.

Conflict between Individual and Job

This type of conflict may occur because of economic pressures to manufacture goods as cheaply as possible. Economies of scale achieved by flow-line and mass production systems have means reducing skill levels of jobs in many instances. The result may be that jobs offer little opportunity for creativity and sense of achievement and this can lead to boredom, frustration and alternation because the needs of the organization's social system are incompatible with those of the technical system. Role conflict can take a number of forms. One example is where the demands of the job exceed the capabilities of the person occupying that position. The occupant may experience role overload where he cannot cope with the physical or mental demands of the job. As a result stress may occur and produce dysfunctional effects which cause problems both for the organization and the individual. In this situation the job may be performed inadequately, the individual may undergo physical or psychological withdrawal and others may have to bear the burdens created by the situation.

A further example of conflict between individual and job is where the individual's capability exceeds the job requirement. As a result, the individual may become bored, disinterest may follow, and alternation may occur with all its associated dysfunctions. Another form of role conflict is that of ambiguity. This may arise either when the individual is unsure of the nature and demands of the job or where there are conflicting demands: possibly where he is responsible to different supervisors for different aspects of his role. As a result he may experience considerable uncertainty and stress and this may in turn give rise to conflict.

To a large extent, conflict arising from overload, underload or ambiguity has a structural basis although personality factors may exacerbate some of the problems.

Conflict between Individuals

This arises when individuals for one reason or another are unable to form satisfactory relationships. This may be due to dissatisfaction with real or imagined status differences, competition for involvement in certain areas of work, competition for resources or personality clashes. To some extent this type of conflict may serve merely as an irritant although if allowed to develop to the point where ill will becomes destructive, it may prove damaging to organization efficiency and effectiveness.

Conflict between individuals can also arise when they operate under different value systems. Some individuals prefer to see themselves as responding purely to the demands of their own set of values. They may resist pressures for conformity brought to bear on them by their colleagues. An example is where an individual refuses to join his colleagues in strike action.

Conflict – A Perspective

Having identified various sources of conflict it is clear that any view of the organization in purely unitary terms is unsatisfactory and misleading. It does not allow for perspectives other than those which support the validity and exercise of traditional management authority. What may be needed are mechanisms for conflict resolution which go beyond those allowed by the unitary approach and which reflect the more genuine reality of polarization of interests. Any attempt to contain conflict by simple authoritarianism may be doomed to failure.

An alternative approach is offered by the pluralist view. This recognizes the existence of many different interest groups with different objectives, influenced by different value systems and working within the power structure of the organization. Conflict resolution is seen as the outcome of a management approach which provides a system of checks and balances. Effectively, it recognizes the legitimacy of all groups to pursue their claims. Trade-off in the form of negotiation ensures a degree of collaboration and may enable individuals and groups to achieve a degree of success in pursuit of their various objectives and goals. For management this implies a gain/loss situation, not in the absolute sense encouraged by the unitary view, but rather in terms of relative gain/loss along a continuum which has minimum and maximum outcomes. Any point of agreement (settlement) along the continuum may be construed as a gain/loss for both sides.

According to the unitary view, conflict has traditionally been seen as something which is harmful and destructive to management authority and control. However, conflict viewed on the basis of the pluralist approach may be seen as a series of interactions between individuals and groups which enable the organization to progress. The interaction provides outcomes which enable stability to be achieved and which provide measures of satisfaction for the participants. In this way conflict may be seen as providing a measure of creativity. Outcomes may represent a basis for establishing new approaches to the question of finding solutions to problems. Fox (1966) Donovan Commission Report provides a useful account of pluralism.

In this light, conflict may be seen to serve the aims of stability and progress. The existence of conflict processes which allow conflict to be managed in this way is a key factor and presents outcomes whereby the various sources of conflict are seen as legitimate and integral parts of the organization system. This is adequately demonstrated in labour relations issues which are managed on the basis of consultancy and negotiation and the conduct of which is regularized to some extent by the existence of rules and procedures.

The pluralist approach has been criticized on the grounds that the actual basis on which negotiation takes place does not, in fact, represent a situation in which both sides have equal status. It is said that management continues to have authority, power and control, even when this is not invoked to its fullest extent, and that management is able to define the boundaries within which negotiation takes place and may thus limit discussion. For example, in wage discussions, debate may be concerned with the amount of the reward (which itself is constrained in various ways), rather than with the basis on which the reward is made.

Critics of the pluralist approach argue that the real substance of industrial conflict is related to the economic and social fabric of society, and that any approach which does not recognize a requirement for fundamental change is, at best, one of simple mediation. As such, the pluralist approach is incapable of resolving conflict. Certainly, this view serves as a reminder of the danger of treating organization issues as though they were totally the outcome of the organization system itself rather than taking a wider viewpoint of the extent of systems boundaries — in this case society itself.

Conflict Management

Ways of dealing with conflict vary according to its nature. Faced with the inevitability of conflict brought about by competition over resources, priorities and objectives and reinforced by individual and group rivalries, organizations attempt to manage this state of affairs in such a way as to achieve at least some degree of integration and conflict resolution. Labour relations are controlled by the processes of industrial bargaining; this recognizes the existence of plurality of interests and of management willingness to acknowledge this state of affairs. This includes both formal and informal bargaining. However, this view may not apply to other issues where management's efforts to retain its prerogative produces at best a benign authority, based on ideas of human relations, but authority nevertheless. This approach focuses on the importance of good communications as an essential element to the clarification of situation in which conflict has occurred. Attention has also been given to the question of giving individuals greater control over what they do, based on notions of participation. The work of McGregor and Likert is of particular significance in this respect.

Conflict between individual and job has also been the subject of considerable attention. We have already mentioned role conflict and its consequences. An increase in division of labour and breakdown of tasks has in many instances resulted in reducing skill levels with consequent deleterious effects on social organization. The search for increasing technical and economic efficiency may have blinded organizations and managers to the need for a compatible social organization, so that technical and social components are viewed and treated as components of the total system. Emery and Trist (1969) have drawn attention to socio-technical systems in which change in any one component may produce change in the others. The existence of jobs with low demands in terms of skill and involvement, and possibly of interest, may offset hoped-for gains arising from technical innovation. In recent years terms such as job enlargement and job enrichment indicate attempts to reverse the trend of reducing skill levels and increasing alienation.

Summary

- Conflict describes situations in which individuals and/or groups of people are in disagreement with each other with the result that inefficiencies or ineffectiveness occur.
- The scale of inefficiency may range from minimal interference to business operations through to the occurrence of serious dysfunctions.
- In the past, management's view of the cause of conflict has been simplistic, encouraged by the perspective offered by classical organization theory and related largely to the breakdown of formal authority and the need for measures which will restore it.

Self-Learning Activity

Try to answer the following questions on your own:

1. Critically discuss conflict between manager and managed.
2. How conflict is managed in organizations?

12
Organization Development

Bennis defines Organizational Developmental (OD) as "a response to change, complex educational strategy intended to change the beliefs, attitudes, values, and structure of organizations so that they can better adapt to new technologies, markets, and challenges and the dizzying rate of change itself".

Essentially OD is a long-range attempt to improve an organization's ability to cope with:

1. changes in its external environment;
2. to improve its internal problem-solving abilities.

In other words OD is designed to integrate the needs, goals and objectives of the organization with the needs of the individual order to encourage his involvement and help his growth and development on the job.

OD stresses the process by which people in organizations become more aware of themselves and others. The emphasis is on the psychological states of employees which inhibit their ability to communicate and interact with other organizational members. The assumption is that organizational effectiveness can be increased if people can engage in honest and open discussion of issues.

Characteristics

1. OD is planned. It is a data-based approach to change which involves all of the ingredients that go into

managerial planning. It involves goal setting, action planning, implementation monitoring, and taking corrective action when necessary.

2. OD is problem-oriented. It attempts to apply theory and research from a number of disciplines, including behavioural science, to the solution of organisation problems.
3. OD reflects a systems approach. It is both system and systematic. It is a way of more closely linking the human resources and potential of an organization to its technology, structure and management processes.
4. OD is an integral part of the management process. It is not something that is done to the organization by outsiders. It becomes a way of managing organizational change processes.
5. OD is not a "FIX -IT" strategy. It reflects a continuous and ongoing process. It is not a series of ad hoc activities designed to implement a specific change. It takes time for it to became a way of life in the organization.
6. OD focuses on improvement. The emphasis of OD is on improvement. It is not just for "Sick" organizations or for "healthy" ones. It is something that can benefit almost any organization.
7. OD is Action-oriented. The focus of OD is on accomplishments and results. Unlike some other approaches to change which tend to describe how organizational change takes place, the emphasis is on getting things done.
8. OD is based upon sound theory and practice. It is not a gimmick. It is solidly based upon the theory and research of a number of disciplines.

The desired organizational outcomes of OD efforts include increased effectiveness, problem-solving and adaptability. For human resource development, OD attempts to provide opportunities to be human and to increase awareness, participation and influence. An overriding goal is to integrate individual and organizational objectives.

A number of characteristics are implied in the definition of O.D. and these characteristics differ substantially from those in a typical training programme. These are as follows:

(i) Focus on the whole organization;

(ii) System orientation;

(iii) Use of a change agency;

(iv) Problem solving;

(v) Experimental learning;

(vi) Group processes;

(vii) Feedback;

(viii) Contingency orientation; and

(ix) Team building

Fig. 12.1

OD Process or Steps in OD Process

OD is a complicated process that tends to take a year or more in an organization and may continue indefinitely. For a programme of this magnitude, top-management's support is essential. There are many different approaches to OD, but a typical complete programme includes the following steps:

1. *Initial diagnosis:* Top management meets with the consultant to determine the type of OD programme that is needed. During this phase the consultant may seek inputs by means of interviews with various persons in the organization.
2. *Data Collection:* Surveys may be made to determine organizational climate and behavioural problems. The consultant usually meet with groups away from work to develop information from questions such as:
   (a) What kinds of conditions contribute most to your job effectiveness?
   (b) What kinds of conditions interfere with your job effectiveness?
   (c) What would you most like to change in the way this organization operates?
3. *Data feedback and confrontation:* Work groups are assigned to review the data collected, to mediate among themselves areas of disagreement, and to establish priorities for change.
4. *Action Planning and Problem-Solving:* Groups use the data to develop specific recommendations for change. Discussion focuses on actual problems in their organization. Plans are specific, including who is responsible and when the action should be completed.
5. *Team Building:* During the entire period of group meetings the consultant encourages the groups to examine how they work together. The consultant helps them see the value of open communication and trust as prerequisites for improved group functioning. Team building may be

encouraged further by having individual managers and their subordinates work together as a team in OD sessions.

6. *Inter-group development:* Following the development of small group teams, there may be development among larger groups comprising several teams.
7. *Evaluation and follow up:* The consultant helps organization to evaluate the results of its OD efforts and develop additional programmes in areas where additional results are needed.

The steps in OD are part of a whole process, so all of them need to be applied if a firm expects to gain the full benefits of OD. A firm that applies only two or three tops, such as diagnosis and team building, is likely to be disappointed with results. However, the whole process can produce quite favourable results.

Goals/Objectives

1. To increase the level of trust and support among organizational members.
2. To increase the incidence of confrontation of organizational problems, both within groups in contrast to "sweeping problems under the rug".
3. To create an environment in which authority of assigned role is augmented by authority based on knowledge and skill.
4. To increase the openness of communications laterally, vertically and diagonally.
5. To increase the level of personal enthusiasm and satisfaction in the organization.
6. To find synergistic (working together; combined or co-ordinated action) solutions to problems with greater frequency. (Synergistic solutions are creative solutions in which 2+2 equals more than 4, and through which all parties gain more through cooperation than through conflict).

7. To increase the level of self and group responsibility in planning and implementation.

Values of OD

In fact, OD is a way of looking at the whole human side of organizational life. The emphasis of OD on human dimensions of organization is reflected in the following cardinal list of humanistic values.

1. Providing opportunities for people to function as human beings rather than as resources in the production process.
2. Providing opportunities for each organization member, as well as for the organization itself, to develop to his full potential.
3. Seeking to increase the effectiveness of the organization in terms of all of its goals.
4. Attempting to create an environment in which it is possible to find exciting and challenging work.
5. Providing opportunities for people in organizations to influence the way in which they relate to work, the organization and the environment.
6. Treating each human being as a person with a complex set of needs, all of which are important in his work and in his life.

Techniques of OD

1. Sensitivity training
2. Team Building
3. Survey feedback
4. Grid training
5. System management
6. Management by objectives (MBO).

Just for understanding, first two techniques are discussed hereunder:

Sensitivity Training

Sensitivity training (sometimes call— group training) is focused on allowing members to become more sensitive to the ways in which they related to others.

It is a small group of 10 to 12 people assisted by a professional behavioural scientist who acts as a catalyst for the group. There is no specified agenda. He merely creates the opportunity for group members to express their ideas and feelings freely. Since the trainer has no leadership role to play, the group must work out its own methods of proceedings. A leaderless and agendum free group session is on. They can discuss anything they like. Individuals are allowed to focus on behaviour rather than on duties. As members engage in the dialogue they are encouraged to learn about themselves as they interact with others.

Team Building

Organizations are made up of people working together to achieve some common end. Since people are frequently required to work in groups, considerable attention has been focused in OD on team building.

Team Building (TB) can be applied within groups or at the inter-group level where activities are interdependent. Not all group activity has interdependence of functions. To illustrate consider a football team and a track team.

Although members of both teams are concerned with the teams' total output they function differently. The football teams' output depends synergistically (combined or coordinated action working together) on how each player does his particular job in concert with his teammates. The quarterbacks' throws the ball, and so as. On the performance is determined largely by a mere addition of the performances of the individual members.

Team building is applicable to the case of inter-dependence, such as in football. The objective is to improve coordinative efforts of team members which will result in increasing the group's performance.

The activities considered in team building typically include goal setting, development of interpersonal relations among team member's, role analysis to clarify each member's role and responsibilities and team process analysis. Of course, team building may emphasize or exclude certain activities depending on the purpose of the development effort and the specific problems with which the team is confronted. Basically, however, team building attempts to use high interaction among group members to increase trust and openness. Team - Building (TB) requires members to:

(i) Learn thoroughly about himself;

(ii) Know and to respect the sentiments of others;

(iii) Learn the principle of mutuality and reciprocity in his behaviour with others; and

(iv) Learn to subordinate personal object to group of objects.

Ways/Approaches to Team Building

1. The consultant will interview members of the team to know their feelings, attitudes and perceptions of team effectiveness. After that the consultant arranges a meeting of the group away from the organization in which the consultant feedbacks the data. Then the set of priorities are worked out and action-plan formulated for resolving' the problems.
2. Each member will discuss with another member his perceived roles and also team feeling so as to make contributions, suggestions or comments more productive

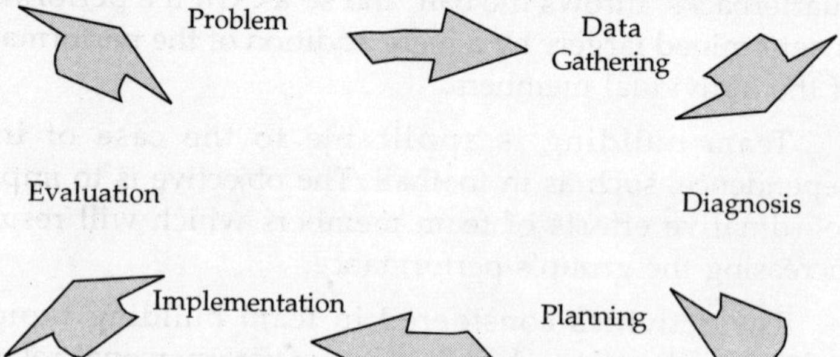

Fig. 12.2: **Team Building Cycle**

and meaningful. The exercise will help in removing most of misunderstandings existing between team members and also to ensure that each team member accepts his role as well as the role of other team members.

Organizational Change

Organizations encounter both external and internal forces for change. There are four key external forces for change: demographic characteristics, technological advancements, market changes, and social and political pressures. Internal forces for change come from both human resource problems and managerial behaviour/decisions.

Lewin developed a three-stage model of planned change that explained how to initiate, manage, and stabilize the change process. The three stages were: unfreezing, which entails creating the motivation to change, changing, and stabilizing change through refreezing. A systems model of change takes a big picture perspectives of change it focuses on the interaction among the key components of change. The three main components of change are inputs, target elements of change, and outputs. The target elements of change represent the components of an organization that may be changed. They include organizing arrangements, social factors, methods, goals, and people.

John Cotter believes that organization change fails for one or more of eight common errors. He proposed eight common errors. He proposed eight steps that organizations should follow to overcome these errors. The eight steps are:

1. Establish a sense of urgency
2. Ereate the guiding coalition
3. Develop a vision and strategy
4. Dommunicate the change vision
5. Empower broad-based action
6. Generate short-term wins
7. Consolidate gains and produce more change
8. Anchor new approaches in the culture.

The identifying characteristic of OD are that it:

(a) involves profound change.

(b) is value loaded.

(c) is a diagnosis/Prescription cycle.

(d) is process oriented.

Resistance to Change

Resistance to change is an emotional/behavioural response to real or imagined threats to an established work routine. Ten reasons employees can resist change are:

1. An individual's predisposition toward change.
2. Surprise and fear of the unknown.
3. Climate of mistrust.
4. Fear of failure.
5. Loss of status or job security.
6. Peer pressure.
7. Disruption of cultural traditions or group relationships.
8. Personality conflicts.
9. Lack of tact of poor timing.
10. Non-reinforcing reward systems.

The first entails an employee's commitment to change, which reflects a mind-set of doing whatever it takes to effectively implement change. Resilience to change, a composite characteristic reflecting high self-esteem, optimism, and an internal locus of control, is the second personal characteristic people with a positive self-concept and a tolerance for risk also handle change better than those without these two dispositions. High levels of self-efficacy also are negatively associated with resistance to change.

Organizations must be ready for change. Assuming an Organization is ready for change, the alternative strategies for overcoming resistance to change are: education + communication, participation + involvement, facilitation +

support, negotiation + implicit coercion. Each has its situational appropriateness and advantages and drawbacks.

Stress

Stress is an adaptive reaction to environmental demands or stressors that triggers a fight or flight response. This response creates hormonal changes that mobilize the body for extraordinary demands. According to the occupational model of stress, the stress process begins when an individual cognitively appraises stressors. This appraisal then motivates an individual to choose a coping strategy aimed at reducing stressors, which, in turn, results in a variety of stress outcomes.

The stress moderators are social support, hardiness, and Type A behaviour. People use each of these moderators to help reduce the impact of stressors that are appraised as harmful, threatening, of challenging. Social support represents the amount of perceived helpfulness derived from social relationships. People use four types of support— esteem, informational, social, and instrumental— to reduce the impact of stress. Hardiness is a collection of personality characteristics that neutralize stress. It includes the characteristics of commitment, locus of control, and challenge. The Type A behaviour pattern is characterized by someone who is aggressively involved in a chronic, determined struggle to accomplish more and more in less and less time. Management can help Type A individuals by not overloading them with work despite their apparent eagerness to take on an ever-increasing workload.

Muscle relaxation, bio-feedback meditation, cognitive restructuring, and a holistic wellness approach are predominating stress-reduction techniques. Slow and deep breathing and a conscious effort to relieve muscle tension are common denominators of muscle relaxation. Bio-feedback relies on a machine to train people to detect bodily signs of stress. This awareness facilitates pro-active coping with stressors. Meditation activities are relaxation response by redirecting one's thoughts away from oneself. Cognitive restructuring entails identifying irrational or mal-adaptive thoughts and replacing them with rational or logical thoughts.

Holistic wellness is a broad, interdisciplinary approach advocating that people strive for personal wellness in all aspects of their lives. The five key components underlying this approach are self-responsibility, nutritional awareness, stress reduction and relaxation, physical fitness, and environmental sensitivity.

Managing Change

Changes are constantly taking place in our environment. For instance, the computer age is transforming the manner in which it is being done in organisations all over the world. John Naisbitt (1982) in his book, *Mega trends*, vividly describes the changes that are transforming society itself. The world is getting smaller and trade and transactions can now be completed in a matter of seconds via high speed telecommunication technology almost all over the universe. It is not merely the technological environment that is changing; the economic, political, market, social, legal and labour environments are also changing. For instance, the young, highly qualified, confident, and spirited professionals of today are not of the same breed as their forebears. New ideas, beliefs, and changes are what keep the wheels of business and industry adapting to the environmental changes and keep them forging ahead.

By being able to scan the internal and external environment of the organisation and deciding how changes in these environments are likely to widen the gap between desired and actual state of affairs (Performance, productivity, customer satisfaction, employee's satisfaction, and the like), the manager can become an effective agent for introducing planned changes.

Planned Change

When changes are effected in a planned manner after assessing the need for change and working out the details of when and how they will be carried out, planned changes occur. This is in contrast to changes that take place in random fashion reactively as crisis situations develop. For pro-active changes to be initiated, the manager should be constantly alert to the changes taking place in the external and internal environments of the organization so that corrective action is taken and successfully carried out, thus averting the frequent occurrence of crisis situations. This implies that managers constantly monitor the various environments that the organization faced and be vigilant boundary spanners.

Introducing Change

The timing and manner in which changes are introduced in a system have a lot to do with how successful the changes become. Changes can be introduced effectively when factors that would be conducive to the acceptance of the changes and the factors that would cause people to resist the change are first identified. Once identified, resistance to change can be decreased in various ways including improving the communication process.

Resistance to Change

Resistance to change is of three different types. These types work in combination to produce each employee's total attitude towards a change.

The three types may be expressed by three different uses of the word "logical", as follows:

- ❖ Logical, based on rational reasoning and science.
- ❖ Psychological, based on emotions, sentiments, and attitudes.
- ❖ Sociological, based on group interest and values.

Logical, rational objections

- ❖ Time required to adjust.
- ❖ Extra efforts to relearn.
- ❖ Possibility of less desirable conditions, such as skill downgrading.

- ❖ Economic costs of change.
- ❖ Questioned technical feasibility of change.

Psychological, emotional attitudes

- ❖ Fear of the unknown.
- ❖ Low tolerance of change.
- ❖ Dislike of management or other change agents.
- ❖ Lack of trust in others.
- ❖ Need for security; desire for status quo.

Sociological factors; group interests

- ❖ political coalitions.
- ❖ Opposing group values.
- ❖ Parochial, narrow outlook.
- ❖ Vested interests.
- ❖ Desire to retain existing friendships.

Logical resistance arises from the time and effort required to adjust to change, including new job duties that must be learned. These are true costs borne by the employees. Even though a change may be favourable for employees in the long run, these short-run costs must first be paid.

Psychological resistance is 'logical' in terms of attitudes feelings of individual employees about change. They may fear the unknown, mistrust. management's leadership, or feel that their security is threatened. Even though management may believe there is justification for these feelings, they are real and must be recognized. Sociological resistance is 'logical' in terms of group interests and values. Social values are powerful forces in the environment, so they must be carefully considered. There are political coalitions, opposing labour union values, and even different community values. On a small group level there are work friendships that may be disrupted by changes.

Employees will ask questions such as: Is the change consistent with group values? Does it maintain group teamwork? Since employees have these kinds of questions in their minds, administrators need to try to make these conditions as favourable as possible if they intend to deal successfully with sociological resistance.

Clearly all three types of resistance must be treated effectively if employees are to accept change cooperatively. If administrators work with only the technical, logical dimension of change, they have failed in their human responsibilities. It can be seen that psychological and sociological resistance are not illogical or irrational, rather, they are logical according to different sets of values. They are based on the tune of a different drummer.

In a typical operating situation, full support cannot be gained for every change that is made. Some moderate support, even opposition can be expected. People are different and will not give identical support to each change. What management seeks is a climate in which people have a positive feeling toward most changes and feel secure enough to tolerate other changes. If management cannot win support, it may need to use authority. However, it must recognize that authority can be used only sparingly. If authority is overused, it eventually will become worthless.

Possible Benefits of Resistance

Resistance is not all it can bring some benefits. Resistance may encourage management to re-examine its change proposals so that it can be more sure they are appropriate. In this way employees operate as a check and balance to assure that management properly plans and implements change. If reasonable employee resistance causes management to screen its proposed changes more carefully then employees have discouraged careless management decisions.

Resistance also can help in identifying specific problem areas where a change is likely to cause difficulties, so that management can take corrective action before serious problems develop. At the same time, management may be encouraged to do a better job of communicating the change, an approach that in the long-run should lead to better acceptance. Resistance also gives management information about the intensity of employee emotions on an issue, provides emotional release for pent-up employee feelings, and may encourage employees to think and talk more about a change so that they understand it better.

Three Steps for Planned Changes

Kurt Lewin, the father of change processes, identified three phases in initiating and establishing any change—unfreezing, changing or moving, and refreezing.

Unfreezing

Unfreezing is actually the process of preparing the system for change through discontinuation of the old practices, attitudes, tendencies, or behaviours. This is the initial phase where those involved in the change experience a need for something different and a sense of restlessness with the status quo. In essence, the feeling that the system is hurting itself badly now and desperately requires a change if it is to survive, is sensed by you. An excellent example of this is the recent hue and cry in the US that the elementary, secondary and high school education in the country desperately needed to be improved: parents, educators, students, the job market, and the society itself was hurting because of the "educated illiterates", that America was producing. Americans feared that the USA will fast become a nation of illiterates who will be unable to contribute to the nation's progress and prosperity if things continued the way they were. The society was hurting so much that it wanted changes in the educational system—better qualified and motivated teachers who would produce competent scholars and not illiterates who have gone through the motions of the educational process without learning anything. The need for change was recognized and desired. The system was unfrozen from its complacency that everything was fine with the pre-college educational system.

Changing or Moving

Changing or moving is the phase where the changes that have been planned are actually initiated and carried out. Changes could relate to the mission, strategy, objectives, people, tasks, work roles, technology, structure, corporate culture, or any other aspect of the organisation. Well thought out changes have to be carefully implemented with the participation of the members who will be affected by the change. Changes incorporated too quickly without adequate preparation will result in resistance to change.

Refreezing

Refreezing is the last phase of the planning change process. Refreezing ensures that the planned changes that have been introduced are working satisfactorily, that any modifications, extra considerations, or support needed for making the change operational are attended and that there is reasonable guarantee that the changes will indeed fill the gap and bring the system to the new, desired state of equilibrium. This necessarily implies that the results are monitored and evaluated, and wherever necessary, corrective measures are taken to reach the new goal. If the refreezing phase is neglected or improperly attended to, the desired results will not ensue and the change may be even a total disaster.

Strategies for Planned Change

Chin and Benne (1976) describe three strategies that managers commonly use to introduce change. They are: empirical-rational, normative-re-educative, and power-coercive.

Empirical-Rational Strategy

Managers who act as change agents might subscribe to the belief that people are rational and if they understand that the change to be introduced will benefit them, their self-interest will react positively to change if the benefits of the change to the individual or the group are properly understood. So, if the manager explains the benefits of change to the employees and then introduces it, it is likely to be a success.

Normative-Re-educative Strategy

In the normative-re-educative strategy the belief is that people are guided by the socio-cultural norms that they subscribe to. Changes do not always take place merely because they make sense to people at the rational or cognitive level but changes become acceptable because they are in-keeping with the personal values and belief system of the people. Thus, 'when changes appeal to the socio-cultural norms of individuals affected by the change, they are successfully implemented. Hence, when the necessary changes to be made are identified, the change agent and those who will be influenced by the change should participatively and collaboratively plan and implement the necessary changes. This will ensure that successful changes occur in the system because people have internalised the need for changes as they worked together in developing and implementing them.

Power-Coercive Strategies

Power-coercive strategies are used by change agents who operate under the assumption that people with less power will comply with the changes brought about by those with more power in the system. This strategy will utilise legitimate authority, rewards, and punishments as means to enforce change. Though people may respond because of fear, they may resist the changes psychologically and react in subtle ways, as discussed earlier. The compliance to any orders imposing changes will be of a temporary nature and once the change agent is out of sight, people will revert to their old ways of doing things.

Change must be Managed

Changes must be planned and actively managed if organizations are to survive and grow. Kanter and Stein (1980) suggest that where large-scale changes are involved, special structures such as a high-level steering committee or advisory group may be necessary to manage the transition. Kanter (1983) states that effective change masters combine a steadfast vision with a willingness to be flexible as they travel the path to reach their goals. Managing change thus becomes an important part of the managerial job. Constantly assessing where we are and where we want to be, alerts managers to the changes that are needed to be embedded in the system. A planned change has then to be carefully worked out to fill the gap. Thereafter, depending on the situational context in which the change has to be embedded, an appropriate strategy to implement the change has to be decided.

Summary

- OD stresses the process by which people in organizations become more aware of themselves and others. The emphasis is on the psychological states of employees which inhibit their ability to communicate and interact with other organizational members.
- Organizations encounter both external and internal forces for change. There are four key external forces for change: demographic characteristics, technological advancements, market characteristics, technological advancements, market changes, and social and political pressures, internal forces for change come from both human resource problems and managerial behaviour/decisions.

Self-Learning Activity

Try to answer the following questions on your own:

1. What are the steps in OD process?
2. Write short notes on Resistance to Change.
3. Describe the strategies for introducing planned change?

References

Ash, M.G. (1992. "Cultural Contexts and Scientific Change in Psychology: Kurt Lewin in Iowa". *American Psychologist*, Vol. 47, No. 2, pp. 198-207.

Bakke, D.W. (2005). *Joy at Work: A Revolutionary Approach to Fun on the Job*. Seattle, WA: PVG.

Carnegie, D. (1979). *Live Enthusiastically*. Garden City, NY: Dale Carnegie & Associates.

Clawson, J.G. (2009). *Level Three Leadership: Getting Below the Surface* (4th ed.). Upper Saddle River, NJ: Pearson Prentice Hall.

EI Framework. (n.d.). "Consortium for Research on Emotional Intelligence in Organizations". Retrieved October 5, 2008, from http://www.eiconsortium.org/pdf/emotional_competence_framework.pdf

George, J.M., & Jones, G.R. (2008). *Understanding and Managing Organizational Behaviour* (5th ed.). Upper Saddle River, NJ: Pearson Prentice Hall.

Goleman, D. (1995). *Emotional Intelligence*. New York: Bantam Books.

Goleman, D. (2004, January). "What Makes a Leader"? [Electronic Version]. *Harvard Business Review*, 82(1), 82-91.

Griffin, R.W., & Moorhead, G. (2007). *Organizational Behaviour: Managing People and Organizations* (8th ed.). New York: Houghton Mifflin Company.

Hatch, M.J., *Organization Theory: Modern, Symbolic, and Postmodern Perspectives*. 2nd Ed. Oxford University Press (2006) ISBN 0-19-926021-4.

Jones, Ishmael, *The Human Factor: Inside the CIA's Dysfunctional Intelligence Culture*. New York: Encounter Books (2008) ISBN 978-1594033827.

Kanigel, R. (1997). *The One Best Way, Frederick Winslow Taylor and the Enigma of Efficiency*. London: Brown and Co.

Kidder, R. M. (2003). *How Good People Make Tough Choices: Resolving the Dilemmas of Ethical Living*. New York: Harper.

Mayer, J., DiPaolo, M., & Salovey, P. (1990, June). "Perceiving Affective Content in Ambiquous Visual Stimuli: A Component of Emotional Intelligence" [Electronic Version]. *Journal of Personality Assessment*, 54(3-4), 772-781.

Peale, N.V. (1967). *Enthusiasm Make the Difference*. New York: A Fawcett Crest Book.

Robbins, S.P., & Judge, T. A. (2008). *Essentials of Organizational Behaviour* (9th ed.). Upper Saddle River, NJ: Pearson Prentice Hall.

Robbins, Stephen P. *Organizational Behaviour — Concepts, Controversies, Applications*. 4th Ed. Prentice Hall (2004) ISBN 0-13-170901-1.

Scott, W. Richard. *Organizations and Organizing: Rational, Natural, and Open Systems Perspectives*. Pearson Prentice Hall (2007) ISBN 0-13-195893-3.

Simon, Herbert A. *Administrative Behaviour: A Study of Decision-Making Processes in Administrative Organizations*, 4th ed. 1997, The Free Press.

Tompkins, Jonathan R. Organization Theory and Public Management.Thompson Wadsworth (2005) ISBN 978-0-534-17468-2.

Weick, Karl E. *The Social Psychology of Organizing*, 2nd Ed. McGraw Hill (1979) ISBN 0-07-554808-9.

Index

A

Age of human and social capital, 33
Aston group and Organization size, 15
Attitude formation, 105
Attitudes and communication, 108
Auburn University, 79
Authority, 133-144

B

Basic psychological process, 35-62
- abilities and performance, 46-47
- abilities, 41-42
- attitudes, 41-42, 44-45
- attribution tendencies, 61-62
- causal attributions, 60-61
- causes and consequences of job satisfaction, 48-50
- four-stage sequence and a working example, 54
- individual differences: self-concept, personality and emotions, 35
- instrumental and terminal values, 42-43
- intelligence and cognitive abilities, 47-48
- job satisfaction, 41-42, 48-50
- key work attitudes, 45-46
- major correlates and consequences of job satisfaction, 50-53, 62
- organizational identification, 37
- personality, 37-41
- self-efficacy, 36
- self-esteem, 35-36
- self-monitoring, 36-37
- social perception, 53-54
- stereotypes, 58-60
- value conflicts, 43
- values, 41-42

Behaviour theory, 141
British Steel Corporation, 135

C

Case for Technology, 15
Chester Barnard and Cooperative Systems, 13
Communication, 94-100
- barriers to communication, 99-100
- communication process, 96-97
- definition, 94
- elements in the process of communication, 94-95
- importance of communication, 95

methods of communication in management, 96

objectives of communication, 96

principles of good communication-7Cs, 97-98

Conflict between formal and informal organization, 149

Conflict between individual and job, 149-150

Conflict between individuals, 150-151

Conflict between manager and managed, 149

Conflict management, 153-154

Contingency theory, 141

Contributing disciplines to the OB field, 22

anthropology, 23

political science, 23

psychology, 22

social psychology, 23

sociology, 22-23

D

Davis, Ralph , 11

Department of Employment, 114

Donovan Commission Report, 152

Doughlas McGregor and Theory X, Theory Y, 13

E

Elton Mayo and the Hawthorne Studies, 12

Employment Protection Consolidation Act (1978), 116

Encoding and simplification, 55

F

Fayol, Henri, 11

Frederick Taylor and Scientific Management, 10

G

Group cohesiveness, 82

Group dynamics, 77-93

adjourning, 82

formal and informal groups, 78

forming, 81

functions of formal groups, 78

group development process, 80-81

groups and social exchanges, 77-78

norming, 81-82

performing, 82

roles and norms, 82

social exchanges in the workplace, 79-80

storming, 81

Groves, Frank , 97

H

Hawthorne Legacy, 32

Hawthorne studies, 30

Henri Fayol and Principles of Organization, 11

Herbert Simon and Principles Backlash, 14

I

Influence, 133-144

K

Katz and Kahn Environmental Perspective, 15

Key work attitudes, 45-46

L

Leadership, 133-144
- characteristics of leadership, 139-140
- definition, 138-139
- goals of leadership, 139

M

Manager as an analyst, 19
Managerial Revolution, 115
March and Simon Cognitive Limits to Rationality, 16
Maslow Theory, 66
Max Weber and Bureaucracy, 11
McGregor, Doughlas ,13
Ministry of Education, 25
Motivation, 63-76
- benefits of motivation, 64-75
- definition, 63-64
- esteem needs, 66
- love and social needs, 65
- motivators, 75-76
- psychological needs, 65
- safety needs, 65
- self-actualisation needs, 66-75

N

National Coal Board, 114
Nature and scope of organizational behaviour, 20
Norms, 85
- how norms are developed, 85-86
- why norms are enforced, 86

O

Ohio State University, 141
Organization conflict, 145-154
- causes of conflict, 146
- conflict between formal and informal organization, 149
- conflict between individual and job, 149-150
- conflict between individuals, 150-151
- conflict between manager and managed, 149
- conflict management, 153-154
- conflict, 151-153
- conflicts between difference departments or groups within the organization, 147-149
- differences between corporate and individual goals, 146-147

Organization control, 120-132
- control and planning, 125-128
- control methods, 121-125
- controlsome considerations, 120-121
- informal relationships, 131-132
- management by objectives, 128-131

Organization development, 155-173
- characteristics, 155-157
- goals/objectives, 159-160
- introducing change, 167
- managing change, 166
- OD process or steps in OD process, 158-159
- organizational change, 163-166
- planned change, 166-167
- possible benefits of resistance, 169-170

resistance to change, 167-169
strategies for planned change, 171-172
techniques of OD, 160
three steps for planned changes, 170
change must be managed, 172-173
changing or moving, 171
refreezing, 171
unfreezing, 170
values of OD, 160
Organization goals, 110-119
goal conflict, 118-119
nature of business organization goals, 113-118
problems of goal identification, 111-113
why organizations have goals, 110-111
Organization structure, 4-5
Organization Theory (OT), 6
Organization, 1-17
contrasting organization theory and organizational behavior, 6-7
evolution of organizational theory, 7-10
organization charts, 3-4
what is an organization design, 5
what is an organization structure, 4-5
centralization, 5
complexity, 5
formalization, 5
what is an organization, 1-3
what is an organizational theory, 6
Organizational behaviour, 6, 18-34
an art or a science, 21
and your career, 24
nature, 20-21
scope, 21-22
Organizational Developmental (OD), 155

P

Path-goal theory, 142
Perception and attitudes, 101-109
Perception process, 101
Pfeffer organizations as political arenas, 16
Power, 133-144
Principles Backlash, 14
Project Evaluation and Review Technique (PERT), 126

R

Ralph Davis and Rational Planning, 11
Retrieval and response, 58
Roles, 82
Asch effect, 88-89
functional roles performed by group members, 86-87
groupthink, 89-91
role ambiguity, 84-85
role conflict, 84
role overload, 84
social loafing, 91-93
threats to group effectiveness, 88

S

Sale of Goods Act (1979), 116

Selective attention/comprehension, 54
Silverman Theory of Organizations (1970), 131
Storage and retention, 56
Systems approach to the study of organization behaviour, 24
    characteristics of an open system, 27-30
    closed system, 25-26
    open system, 26-27
    types of systems, 25

T

Taylor, Frederick, 10
Theories of perception, 104
Theory X, 13
Theory Y, 13
Trait theory, 140

U

U.S.A., 170

V

Vroom-Yetton model, 143

W

Warren Bennis and the Death of Bureaucracy, 14
Western Electric Company, 31
Williamson Management Discretion Theory (1967), 116
Workplace Social Exchange Network (WSEN), 79

Hindu Mysticism Philosophy & Religion

(According to the Upaniṣads)

(Revised and Enlarged Edition)